A History of
ENGLISH
GLASSMAKING
AD 43-1800

A History of
ENGLISH
GLASSMAKING
AD43-1800

HUGH WILLMOTT

TEMPUS

First published 2005

Tempus Publishing Limited
The Mill, Brimscombe Port,
Stroud, Gloucestershire, GL5 2QG
www.tempus-publishing.com

British Library Cataloguing in Publication Data.
A catalogue record for this book is available from the British Library.

ISBN 0 7524 3131 5

Typesetting and origination by Tempus Publishing Limited
Printed in Great Britain

CONTENTS

PREFACE AND ACKNOWLEDGEMENTS

The English glass industry has been the subject of a number of excellent historical and archaeological studies over the last century. However, the lack of a synthesis of this material, especially one taking the longer-term view, has been apparent for some time. This book is an attempt to bring together into one place the wide range of sources for the industry for the best part of two millennia. Perhaps predictably, such an approach is not unproblematic.

Firstly, it is too easy for the author to appear to take credit for all the work covered. Inevitably this book is largely based on the research and efforts of other scholars, while the author has only contributed small amounts of original material. In the course of the collation of all the data presented here, it is hoped that suitable recognition has been paid to others, either in the acknowledgements, or the figure captions, or in the text itself. It is also for this reason that a comprehensive bibliography is included at the end. This book is intended to be a general introduction to the topic, but it should certainly not be considered the final word on it.

A second flaw with this synthesis is that there has been a process of selection in what material to include, which inevitably leads to certain biases. For this reason the study ends somewhat artificially at around 1800. While it might have been appropriate to continue until the present day, there simply is not the space in a single book to do justice to the material. Given the massive expansion that occurred in the industry from the early years of the nineteenth century, coupled with the technological changes that occurred, it seemed appropriate that these should be subject to a separate study. Likewise it might be thought that this book is rather Anglo-centric. However, Scotland is not dealt with here as, prior to 1610, there was no production north of the border, and the later industry recently has been comprehensively analysed in Jill Turbull's *The Scottish Glass Industry 1610-1750*, and there is no need to replicate this excellent work.

Many people deserve specific mention as, without their help or forbearance, this book could never have been written. First and foremost my thanks go to Peter Kemmis Betty and the Tempus team, who coped with my inability to keep to a deadline with remarkably good humour. I am indebted to Antonia Thomas, who prepared most of the first drafts of the line drawings, while Mark Eccleston and Kate Welham provided many useful comments on earlier drafts of the text. More general discussions with Caroline Jackson, Jennifer Price and Kieron Tyler helped refine many of my ideas over the industry, its mechanics and development. I am particularly grateful too to David Crossley, who provided advice and also allowed me to freely reproduce photographs from his many glasshouse excavations, while Andrew Smith was generous in allowing me access to his unpublished research. I shall always remember the afternoon spent at the Corning Museum of Glass with Bill Gudenrath, replicating different types of waste, I am still amazed how much I learnt in a few hours. My final thanks must, however, go to all those historians and archaeologists past and present, without whose efforts this book could not have been written. In particular this book is dedicated to the late Denis Ashurst, whose meticulous excavation and methodical research set a level of scholarship rarely met by more established academics.

1

INTRODUCTION: THE NATURE AND FORMATION OF GLASS

GLASS AS A SUBSTANCE

On one hand, glass is often taken for granted as a simple everyday material, used for the most mundane of objects, and yet on the other it is often assumed to be modern medium, particularly when associated with contemporary architecture or fibre-optic technologies. Both assumptions are, in fact, incorrect; glass is both incredibly complex compositionally and has had a history of production that stretches over 4,000 years.

Glass does appear in certain circumstances as a natural substance, most prominently on Melos in the Aegean and the Lipari Islands in the Mediterranean, where geothermic processes associated with sudden volcanic eruptions fused natural sands into a dark black glass known as obsidian. Another similar, if less common, source of natural glass is lechatelierite, formed by lightning striking the desert, causing a natural fusion of the sand. Prehistoric societies exploited both these sources in the same way they did flint, making tools by knapping the glass into the desired shape.

Defining what glass is is surprisingly complex and it is only in the last sixty years or so that its physical properties have been fully understood. Perhaps the best definition of what constitutes glass came from the late Roy Newton, who described it as a 'fusion of inorganic material that has been cooled to a hard condition without crystallisation taking place'. In the case of obsidian and lechatelierite, the inorganic material being fused was just sand (and any accidental impurities present), but this requires a minimum temperature of 1,720°C, a heat that was very hard for most early societies to replicate. Consequently all historical glasses have other ingredients added into the batch that is to be melted.

The most important of these is known as a network modifier or 'flux', and this usually takes the form of an alkaline salt. The purpose of the flux is to interact with the silica network of the glass, breaking down some of the ionic bonds and resulting in the fusion of the glass at a lower, more achievable, temperature. In various periods and different geographical locations, a variety of alkalis were used. Some of the first exploited were oxides of sodium, either as sodium carbonate (Na_2CO_3) or sodium nitrate ($NaNO_3$). In the ancient world the prime sources were natural deposits of evaporated seawater, the largest of these being the Wadi Natrum in Egypt. Sodium oxide could also be made by burning and ashing certain salt marsh plants, usually of the genus *salicornia*, which include seaweeds commonly found in most coastal areas. The second major source of alkali, particularly from the Middle Ages onwards, came from potash derivatives. Perhaps, with access to the traditional sodium-based sources being disrupted, glassmakers started to use alkalis made from burnt plant ashes. These are often thought to have come from beech wood, but other trees could also have been used, as well as bracken (*colour plate 1*). When turned into ash and added to the silica, a potasso-calcic glass was formed, high in potassium oxide (K_2O).

From the later seventeenth century onwards a further network modifier was also added to glass in the form of lead oxide. Two different oxides were most commonly used: litharge (PbO) and red lead (Pb_3O_4). Lead oxides had to be used in conjunction with other alkalis (otherwise the glass would become unstable and 'crizzle') and this was usually potash-based. However, the addition of lead oxide had the effect of producing a brighter glass with a higher refractive index more suited to cutting, and one that was tougher and less likely to shatter.

As well as containing an alkali, all historical glasses have other ingredients added to them. One that was particularly important for soda-based glasses (although less so for potash and lead glasses) was the inclusion of a stabiliser. Glasses made from sand and sodium oxide are not only unstable when cooled, and often do not retain their shape, but are also soluble in water. To counteract these problems calcium oxide (CaO_2) in the form of lime was added to the batch.

When made from the above ingredients most glasses, while being translucent, will usually have a distinctive green or brown colouration, the strength of which depends on the purity of the ingredients used. The prime reason for this is the accidental, but inevitable, inclusion of iron oxides in the silica sources that cause the natural colouration. Consequently, for a clear glass to be produced, the glassmaker had to add further ingredients. Certainly by the first century AD the Romans had perfected decolourising glass through the introduction of antimony oxide (Sb_2O_3), and by the Middle Ages manganese oxide (MnO) was also used. However, it is virtually impossible to remove all colour from glass, even today. When a modern pane of apparently 'colourless' window glass is examined edge-on it clearly has a green tint to it.

Just as glassmakers sought to remove colour, they also intentionally added it. This technology and the ingredients used probably had their origin in the early glazing of pots or use of decorative enamels on metalwork. As with decolourising, metal oxides were used. Because the metals did not dissolve in the glass they were held in suspension, and this is what caused the optical effect of colour. The most common metals utilised were copper, iron and manganese, their various proportions and the furnace conditions determining the final colouration. In a similar fashion, glassmakers also sometimes sought to deliberately remove the translucent quality of glass through the addition of opacifiers, particularly to produce a white glass. For this purpose tin oxide (SnO_2) was added, although from the eighteenth century onwards arsenic was also used.

THE MANUFACTURE AND MANIPULATION OF GLASS

General Techniques of Glass Production

Although glass today can be made relatively simply and rapidly, historically this was not always the case. One major difference is in the quality and measured quantification of the ingredients. While the modern glassmaker can rely upon pure refined chemicals and raw materials, and has the ability to measure these ingredients precisely to the nearest gram, this was never the case in antiquity. Raw materials, such as sand, often had to be sourced locally and, although they could be refined and cleaned in an attempt to reduce contamination, there was not the degree of standardisation that is found in modern materials. Likewise, prior to the sixteenth century there were no set recipes for glassmaking and, even with the first published texts the exact quantities of ingredients were not properly specified. Consequently the manufacture of glass in the past relied upon the extensive experience, skill and experimentation of the glassmaker, as well as no small element of luck.

Unlike today, it is usually thought that historical glasses had to be made in a two-step process. This was principally for two reasons. The first was that early glassmakers could not achieve the temperatures in their furnaces to fully fuse the ingredients into a homogenous glass in one go (a process that requires a temperature in excess of 1,000°C). Instead, a first step known as fritting was required. During this process the ingredients were gently heated together at a lower temperature of around 700°C. This allowed a solid-state reaction, rather than complete vitrification, to occur between the alkali and the silica. The resulting frit was a friable granular substance that could then be cooled, ground into a fine powder and then remelted at a higher temperature to produce a fine even glass. Experimental frits made from a variety of plant ashes and conforming to medieval recipes have been recreated by Caroline Jackson and Kate Welham, and these turn out to be a white or sometimes light purple granular material (*colour plate 1*) that are remarkably similar to material identified archaeologically as frit. The second reason for fritting was that it allowed for the removal of many of the inherent impurities within the glass, either through the escape of gasses that might otherwise become trapped as air bubbles, or as solid masses when the frit was subsequently crushed.

There is a good argument that fritting was not a necessary practice if the furnace used to melt the ingredients was sufficiently well-built to produce the temperatures required for an effective melt in a single action. This is probably true but, from where evidence survives it seems that fritting was a usual stage in the process in most periods. Certainly medieval glassmaking accounts, such as Theophilus's twelfth-century *De Diversis Artibus*, mention the process, as do later post-medieval sources including Diderot and l'Alembert's *Encyclopédie ou Dictionnaire Raisonné des Sciences, des Arts et des Métiers*, published in twenty-eight volumes between 1751-72.

While it is fairly certain that, for many periods, a stage of fritting was undertaken, the exact way this was done is often less clear. Some historical sources suggest that the frit had to be stirred to avoid it fusing into a semi-vitrified mass, and therefore this has led to the suggestion that the raw materials had to be fritted in large shallow pans to facilitate this. Certainly it seems unlikely that deep and narrow crucibles would have been. Where fritting took place is uncertain in almost all periods. It is usually assumed to have been in either a separate furnace to the melting one, or within a specialist compartment of the main furnace. Up until the medieval period the latter seems to have been the case, although from the seventeenth century onwards a separate structure is more likely; indeed Diderot even illustrates one in his *Encyclopédie* (1). In this case the frit was heated and stirred directly on the furnace shelf and not in a tray or any other container.

Once the frit was heated long enough for a sufficient reaction to have taken place, it was cooled and crushed into a fine powder. This was then ready to be heated in the main melting furnace in specially designed pots or crucibles. The form of both the crucible and the furnace varied enormously through the various periods that glass was produced, and there is no standardised pattern for either. However, for an effective melt of the frit, it is usually acknowledged that the furnace had to reach temperatures of at least 1,000°C and preferably a few hundred degrees more than this. One way that the glassmaker could achieve a more effective melt was by adding broken glass, usually referred to as cullet,

1 A fritting oven as depicted
in Diderot and l'Alembert's
L'Encyclopédie

to the batch in the crucible at this stage. Not only did this have the obvious benefit of recycling old glass and therefore requiring fewer raw ingredients, it also had the effect of lowering the overall melting temperature of the batch. It was also at this stage that any colourants and other ingredients could be added.

Again, the length of time required to fully melt the batch into a workable glass probably varied from furnace to furnace, as well as being dependant upon the capacity of the different crucibles. However, it would certainly have taken a number of hours, during which time the mixture would have had to be regularly stirred to ensure that an homogeneous melt was achieved. Only once this had happened was the glass ready to be formed into the required shape.

The final stage in almost all glass manufacture occurs after the glass has been manipulated into its final form. When glass cools rapidly natural stresses occur in various components, particularly those of differing thickness. If allowed to happen this leaves the glass much weakened and prone to spontaneous shattering. As a consequence glassmakers learnt that their products had to be cooled gently to prevent the build-up of such stresses, a process known as annealing. This usually took place in an annealing oven, sometimes known as a lehr, specifically designed for this process, that could be attached to the main melting furnace or could be a separate structure.

Forming Vessels

Being a highly fluid substance, glass could be, and was, manipulated into an incredible variety of shapes. Prior to the first century BC glass vessels were made either by core-forming, where trails of molten glass were looped around a clay former, much like building a coil pot, or by casting solid blocks that could then be laboriously ground down to form a vessel. However, by the time glass production was introduced into England in the first century AD, almost all glass was formed by blowing, using a hollow tube or blowing iron. It is interesting to note that, until the nineteenth century, almost all glass was free-blown and manipulated by hand, usually involving a small group of people, and virtually all the tools of the trade used by an early Victorian glassmaker would have been immediately recognisable to their Roman counterpart.

Although the types of vessel that could be produced were virtually limitless, there were only a limited variety of processes of manipulation that could be used to achieve these. Most can be identified through the examination of the finished products themselves that display the marks and signs of how they were made. Interestingly though, and of particular relevance to understanding the archaeological remains of furnace and working sites, is that, during the course of producing different types and shapes of vessel, tell-tale shapes of waste were also created. While most of these would have been remelted and are now lost, others inevitably escaped notice or were discarded.

In simplistic terms, vessel manufacture and the associated waste can be divided into three broad categories, although other variations inevitably occur. The first of these is the production of simple 'closed' vessels, made from a single bubble of glass, and typically these are bottles or similar containers. The blowing iron is dipped into the crucible and a blob of glass, known as a gather, is taken onto the end. The glassmaker then inflates this by blowing down the tube to form a bubble, or paraison, of glass that can be manipulated. This might involve rolling the paraison on a smooth surface or block, a processes known as marvering, until something approximating the final shape is achieved (2). At this stage the blowing iron is normally at the top or rim end of the vessel and a second solid iron rod, known as a

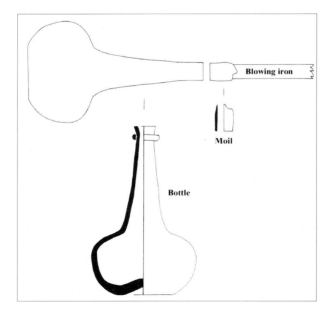

2 Manufacturing a 'closed' vessel.
Author

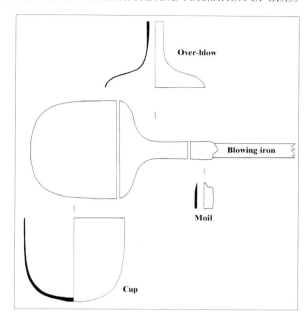

3 Manufacturing an 'open' vessel.
Author

pontil, is applied to the opposing end so that the vessel can be removed from the blowing iron. In the production of such a vessel relatively little waste is produced. The only piece that is usually found is the piece of glass that remains attached to the blowing iron once the closed vessel has been removed, and this is known as the moil.

The second general type of vessel manipulation is in the formation of 'open' vessels made from a single bubble or paraison of glass, and these are typically forms such as simple beakers or cups. In this case a wide mouth is required, so once the general shape has been formed, (with the pontil iron being attached to the base and the blowing iron removed), the extraneous element of glass, known as the over-blow, is removed (*3*). This is achieved once the vessel has cooled somewhat, by either scoring with a flint a horizontal line or by applying a hot trail around the vessel. Both these processes create a stress in the glass, allowing the over-blow to be tapped off. The rim of the vessel is then either briefly heated to round it off, or ground flat.

The third common type of waste is formed when a compound vessel is made from more than one paraison of glass. A typical example might be a footed cup or goblet shape. To produce the upper portion or bowl for such a shape a paraison of glass is blown. However, as the apex of the bubble (the section that is subsequently to be joined to the stem) is naturally the part that is the thickest when blown, this is often thinned out by rolling the paraison between a pair of 'jacks' or sprung pincers (*4*). This reduces the mass of glass at this end, but produces a bulb of excess glass called the paraison end, which is then snipped off before the whole bowl is added to the stem. Another piece of waste is also created in this process. Once the bowl portion has been added to the stem (which is secured on a pontil iron) and the blowing iron removed, the eventual rim needs to be formed. This is done by opening out the edge, rather than tapping off the over-blow. Initially the edge is cut with a pair of shears to remove any excess glass and this creates a ribbon of waste with a characteristic rough edge on one side only where it has been trimmed. The glassmaker then takes the jacks and, while rotating the glass horizontally, uses these to open out the rim until it is the final required shape (*5*).

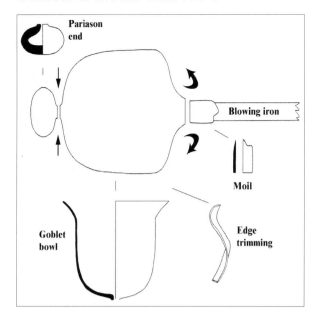

4 Manufacturing a 'compound' vessel. *Author*

5 Opening-out a rim with a pair of jacks. *HMSO*

While these different methods of glass manipulation can create very specific types of leftover glass, the general process of glassblowing creates more generic waste. The excavation of any archaeological glassmaking site reveals that the process was at times quite a messy one: things typically found are drops, runs and splats of glass that have spilt from the crucible or fallen from the end of the blowing iron before the vessel is formed. Indeed, the very process of blowing and manipulating hot paraisons of glass creates tiny threads of glass that can often only be seen microscopically. Furthermore, when the glass was melted in the crucible, impurities often rose to the surface to form a scum or gall that the glassmaker scooped off and discarded.

Forming Window Glass

Window glass was an equally important product through all glassmaking periods in England, although the methods used to make it varied through time. However, in general terms three different processes were employed. The earliest form of window glass introduced by the Romans was made by casting. Molten glass was simply poured onto a bed of sand, allowed to cool a little so it was relatively plastic and then pulled at the edges to form a rectangular sheet of the required size. This type of window glass was consequently quite thick and can be easily identified through having a roughened lower surface where the glass was in contact with the sand.

While predominately a Roman technique, an interesting variation of casting was used from the early seventeenth century onwards, not for window but for mirror and plate glass production. Glass was cast in large sheets in stone or even metal troughs to form a blank, and once this had cooled both surfaces were polished using a succession of finer abrasives to produce a high-quality glass that was thicker than that achieved through blowing. This thick plate glass was soon found to be suited to purposes other than for mirrors that required a stronger material, and cast plate glass was used for coach and ship windows.

Casting, while a sufficient method for producing small sheets, did not allow for the production of particularly transparent windows, and it is not surprising that during the medieval period other methods were adopted. One of the most prevalent of these was through the production of crown glass. The glassmaker took a gather of glass on the end of his blowing iron and inflated this into a large bubble, which he then flattened so that a solid circle of glass was formed. The blowing iron could then be rapidly rotated horizontally so that through centrifugal force a fine disc was formed (6). This could then be cut into quarries, or individual panes, of the required size.

6 Crown glass manufacture as depicted in Diderot and l'Alembert's *L'Encyclopédie*

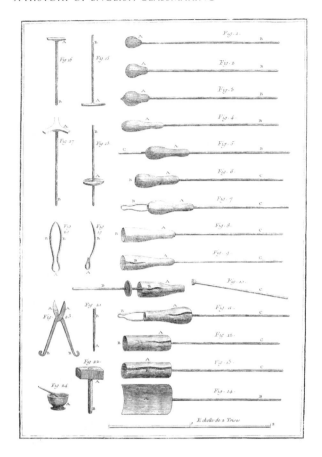

7 Broad glass manufacture as depicted in Diderot and l'Alembert's *L'Encyclopédie*.

The last technique for producing window glass was the cylinder or broad glass method. In this case the glassmaker inflated a large bubble that was then elongated by a combination of inflating and swinging the blowing iron into a long 'sausage' shape (7). This was then allowed to cool slightly before being cut down the centre and opened out into a single large sheet. While cast window glass is distinctive, telling small fragments of crown and cylinder glass apart can be difficult. Both are normally very fine, only a couple of millimetres thick, and often the only way to distinguish between them is the orientation of the air bubbles. Crown glass will have bubbles stretched into circular arrangements, while cylinder glass has elongated parallel rows.

2

ROMAN BEGINNINGS AD 43-500

GLASS IN PREHISTORIC BRITAIN

Before the first legion arrived glass was a rare, but not unknown, sight in Britain. From as early as the Bronze Age small plain decorative beads are sometimes found in barrow burials and even the occasional bracelet is known. However, given the scarcity of these finds they are only likely to have been occasional imports from the Continent. Furthermore, the presence of often no more than a single bead in burials, together with other high-status items, indicates that they were cherished and highly prized.

During the Iron Age beads become more frequent finds, but are still not common on all sites. During this period their designs became much more complex, often consisting of a number of colours in a variety of designs (*8*). Given that these beads are often found at coastal sites known to have been trading with the Continent, such as at Hengistbury Head in Dorset, it suggests that they were still an important trade item. Less clear is whether they might have been manufactured this side of the channel. The technology required was certainly simple: collected fragments of broken vessels, or cullet, could

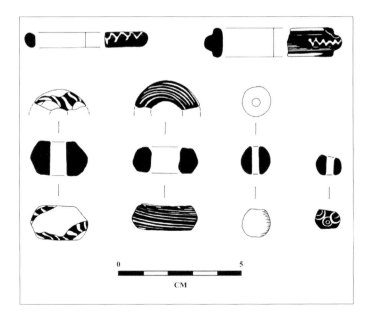

8 Iron Age beads and bangles found at Hengistbury Head. *After Cunliffe*

be melted over an open hearth in simple pots. Nevertheless, to what extent this was occurring is unclear and the archaeological evidence is highly ephemeral.

It is also known that glass was one of a number of commodities exported by Rome to the friendly client kingdoms beyond the edges of its borders. Writing at the end of the first century BC, the Greek geographer Strabo specifically mentioned that ὑαλά σκείη were exported to Britain, where they were clearly prized objects. Sometimes interpreted as 'glass beads' this phrase more accurately translates as 'glass vessels' and finds from archaeological sites have borne this literary evidence out to a certain degree. For example, excavations undertaken within the massive earthwork complex at Stanwick, North Yorkshire, long associated with the tribe of the Brigantes and their pro-Roman Queen Cartimandua, have revealed large numbers of imported goods including prismatic glass bottles.

In spite of the presence of beads and even a very limited number of imported vessels on some high-status sites, Britain was still a virtual stranger to glass by the time of the Claudian invasion in AD 43. However, within just a few years this was to change as a new industry was rapidly introduced, heralding the first sustained period of glass production and use in England.

THE INTRODUCTION OF PRODUCTION

With the arrival of the Roman army and its relatively rapid advance north, a number of new, or at least improved, technologies were introduced. Although ceramics had been made here for several millennia, new kiln technology allowed far better-quality vessels to be made. Furthermore, Iron Age Britain had developed a specialised and highly artistic metalworking industry; with Roman technologies came the ability to mass-produce items. Consequently, while Iron Age communities had mastered many crafts and industries, what the Empire was brought was the apparatus and the will to exploit these, with the initial impetus coming from the army.

It has long been recognised that the army was responsible for many industrial activities early on in the life of the new province of Britannia, and this conformed to the well-established pattern of conquest and Romanisation. While undertaking and controlling industrial production had obvious fiscal, political and even social benefits, it is unlikely that these were the initial impetus for the role the army took in manufacturing. First and foremost the army was the largest consumer of goods in early Roman Britain, and what the legions required had to either be produced locally or more expensively imported from abroad. Consequently it made far more sense for the army to produce as many of its own goods as possible, on one hand saving limited financial resources, but also ensuring a controlled supply of items that were vital to the day-to-day existence of the legions.

Not only did the active role of the army in industrial production make strategic sense, it was an ideal way to promote the spread of new technologies. While it is well recognised that legions themselves were made up of people from all over the Empire, what is more often overlooked is that the army consisted of individuals with diverse skills drawn from across most of the known world. Glassmaking, among other expertises, was not originally native to Britain or any of her immediate neighbours, but with the arrival of the army practiced experts were immediately placed at the heart of Britannia. It was therefore inevitable, rather than just a matter of chance, that glassmaking became so quickly established in the first century AD.

This association of the army with industrial processes can be seen archaeologically, with many production sites being associated with forts. A typical example can be seen at Templeborough, South Yorkshire, where excavations just prior to the First World War revealed the remains of a small glass furnace in the *vicus*, or attached settlement, of the Flavian fort (*9*). Obviously glassmaking was not the only industrial activity undertaken by the army, and it is therefore no surprise that furnaces have been found in areas of more general and mixed industrial production. Perhaps the best example of this can be seen just beyond the confines of the fort at Mancetter, in Warwickshire. A glass furnace and associated working waste dating to the second half of the second century was found to be operating in among a group of pottery kilns. This pattern of mixed industrial quarters in close association to forts is mirrored at other sites across the Western Empire.

However, what is clear is that glassmaking was not only being undertaken at military sites. Indeed there is probably more evidence from Britain of glassmaking being practised on civilian settlements, and more specifically in towns. Placing production sites close to, but often just outside of, the flourishing towns of Britannia made sense. The growing urban populations of the first and second-century province were a clear market for any products and the positioning of furnaces as close as possible to these inevitably reduced transportation costs and the possibility of accidental breakage through carriage. The main difference with urban-centred production was that it was less likely to have been undertaken by the army directly, although as many towns were closely associated with forts they still remained a likely consumer. Clearly glassmaking was an activity undertaken by civilians, although who these were in Britannia is less certain. It has been suggested that many industries in Roman Britain were largely undertaken by

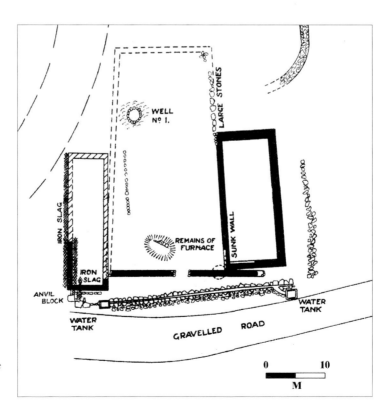

9 The location of the glass furnace within the *vicus* at Templeborough fort. *May*

slaves. However, evidence from other provinces, and epigraphic inscriptions in particular, suggest otherwise. For example the lengthy epitaph of Iulius Alexandrius on a third-century tombstone from Lyon records that he was an *artis vitriae* or 'maker of glass' (*colour plate 2*). He lived to the ripe old age of seventy-five and is described as an excellent man, being blessed with a maidenly wife, four children and seven grandchildren; all desirable 'Roman' qualities. Yet, despite having worked in Lyon, he is recorded as being Carthaginian by birth. This stone indicates that glassmakers could, far from being slaves, afford to commemorate themselves in such a way and had the desire to do so. Furthermore, in the case of Iulius Alexandrius, here was a man who not only had the specialist skills required to make glass, he was willing to travel across the Empire to exploit them. It is by no means inconceivable that there were many other such craftsmen operating in Britain with ethnic backgrounds as diverse as Iulius.

ROMAN PRODUCTION TECHNIQUES

Traditionally Roman glassmaking has been divided into two different manufacturing stages: primary and secondary production. Primary production is the stage of glassmaking where the raw ingredients were initially processed, mixed and melted to form glass, usually with a fitting stage. Secondary production, by contrast, is the formation and shaping of vessels and windows through the melting of pre-prepared glass. The division of the Roman industry into these two phases, particularly by English scholars, has been for two main reasons. Firstly, initial examination of the surviving evidence has led to the suggestion that the only physical remains for the melting of glass from raw ingredients can be found in the Eastern Mediterranean and the Syro-Palestine region in particular. This has been supported by evidence from the scientific analysis of fully formed glasses found archaeologically, which have a far more homogeneous compositional consistency than might be expected if glass was being made from raw ingredients in many different locations across the Empire. Secondly, it has been argued that the apparent lack of evidence for primary glass production in the Western Empire, through the lack of suitable furnaces and other remains, represents genuine evidence of absence for these activities taking place. Both assumptions, while possibly true, should be questioned.

PRIMARY PRODUCTION IN THE EASTERN EMPIRE

The Middle East contains a number of sites that, on the face of it, provide convincing evidence for large-scale primary glass production in the Roman period. It cannot be doubted that the region was a significant area in terms of the industry; the current evidence for the earliest glass-blowing comes from the first half of the first century BC in Jerusalem, and this process was probably first exploited by Syrian workshops shortly after. This, coupled with the evidence for large-scale primary production, has inevitably lead to the assumption that this region was the centre of the Roman industry.

But what is the evidence for primary production in the Roman period? Most often quoted are the impressive series of seventeen tank furnaces excavated at Bet Eli'ezer in Israel. These take the form of large mudbrick-built rectangular features approximately 2m by 4m in size. Although the archaeological remains, due to their structure, are very ephemeral, it would appear the raw materials were placed in the rectangular area and then heated, probably for many days, by an attached firing chamber. This produced a large block of fused glass in one step, without the use of a fritting stage. A large block of glass of similar proportions and weighing over nine tons has been found in a cave at Bet She'arim, Israel. This has been interpreted as a failed firing from such a tank furnace, which was abandoned as it had failed to fuse properly. More tentative evidence for primary production in the region has come in the form of large broken-up blocks of glass found at Taposiris Magna and the Wadi el-Natrun in Egypt.

While these appear to be convincing evidence for large-scale primary production, there are distinct problems with their chronology. The seventeen furnaces from Bet Eli'ezer are well-dated to the six and seventh centuries AD, while it has been suggested that the glass block from Bet She'arim is in fact early Islamic and datable to the ninth century AD. The remains from Taposiris Magna and the Wadi el-Natrum are thought to belong to the Roman period, but await more comprehensive publication. Consequently, as yet there is not the level of evidence for large-scale tank furnace production between the first and fifth centuries AD in the Middle East that might be expected if the region was supplying the whole Empire. This is not to say that glass was not produced in this area at this time and in this way, but its exclusivity of production can be questioned.

SECONDARY PRODUCTION IN THE WESTERN EMPIRE

The suggestion that Roman glass was produced in the Middle East and then transported widely as a raw material for secondary working has been convincingly supported by the occurrence of the glass blocks on shipwrecks in many locations throughout the Mediterranean. Lumps of glass, perhaps used as convenient ballast as well as a trade item, have been recovered from wrecks dating to between the first and fourth centuries, but the most impressive is the late first-century AD wreck off Mljet, Croatia. Rather than being a small additional item of cargo, this particular vessel was carrying over 100kgs of blue/green glass, suggesting it was one of the most important items on its manifest. However, these shipwrecks only confirm that there was a trade in a certain amount of glass, rather than wholesale shipping from East to West.

The evidence for possible secondary production in the Western Empire is quite extensive, with a number of sites in the Northern Provinces containing good furnace remains. Perhaps of particular note are those from the Rhineland. Excavations in 1964 at Nos 35-37 Eigelstein, Cologne revealed the remains of eleven furnaces (*10*). Despite being an obvious sequence of rebuilds on top of each other, all the furnaces were found in pre-Claudian levels, thus dating them to the earlier period of Cologne's occupation. Interestingly two different types can be identified. The first, of which there were five examples, were circular structures with an internal diameter of no more than 1m at most, and often rather less. Similar first-century furnaces from Avenches in modern-day Switzerland suggest that these circular structures often had small square fireboxes to their front. The second type of furnace from Cologne, of which there were six examples, was rectangular in form, measuring approximately 70cm by 90cm. Interestingly, evidence from this site and elsewhere suggests that this second rectangular furnace used a large rectangular crucible that was permanently fixed to the furnace, rather than a smaller removable one. Particularly well-preserved examples from Bonn show that these could be made using large tiles to form the base, and had slab-built clay sides, possibly suggesting that they had a specialised function (*11*). Furthermore, it is important to note that, while at Cologne there were several phases of rebuilding, the different shapes of

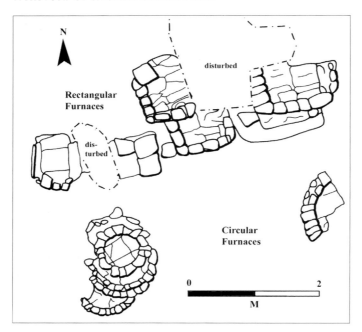

10 Furnaces excavated at Eigelstein, Cologne. *After Follman-Schulz*

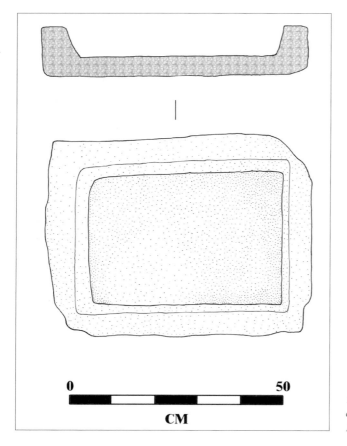

11 Rectangular 'tank' style crucible from Bonn. *After Follman-Schulz*

furnaces always seem to have been built on top of others of similar form. This indicates that at any one time there was always one rectangular and one circular furnace operating together, suggesting that each had a different function.

THE ARCHAEOLOGICAL EVIDENCE FROM ENGLAND

There is a reasonable quantity of evidence for glassworking in Roman Britain (12) and its association with military and urban sites has already been discussed. The archaeological evidence generally falls into three categories: actual furnaces, the remains of crucibles and blowing waste.

Furnaces have been found on a number of archaeological sites in Roman Britain. However, many of these were early in the twentieth century, when excavation and recording techniques were not as well developed as today, leading at times to a rather partial picture of production. Interestingly, with a single exception from Caistor that appears to be rectangular, all other furnaces excavated so far are small and circular. Some, such as one from Castor, Water Newton, excavated in 1828 were not sufficiently recorded for proper comparison. Likewise, excavations undertaken between 1895-1906 at the settlement of Wilderspool, Lancashire by Thomas May revealed the remains of five sub-circular features interpreted as glass furnaces, but from the surviving photographs this interpretation cannot be confirmed (13). However others, such as an example excavated

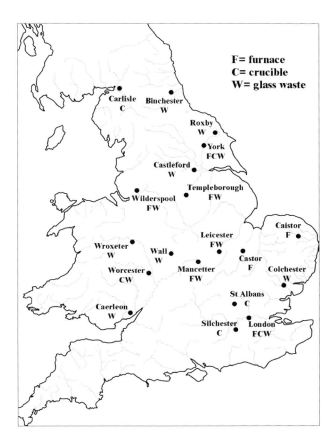

12 Location of evidence of glassmaking in Roman Britain. *Adapted from Price*

13 The Wilderspool furnace. *May*

by John Wacher in 1958 at Blue Boar Lane in Leicester, is much more complete (*colour plate 3*). Dating to the late third century this furnace was dug into the ground surface and lined with flat stones, having an internal diameter of approximately 80cm. In front of an opening into the furnace was a shallow scoop, and this probably was the remains of an external firebox, resembling the round furnaces of Cologne and Avenches.

In common with many continental parallels, only the very lowest portions of the Wilderspool and Leicester furnaces survive. As such, their full reconstruction is difficult and other sources are helpful in this regard. Unlike later periods, very few depictions of glass furnaces survive from the Roman period. One comes from three late first-century pottery lamps made in variations of the same poor-quality low-relief mould. Two examples found in Dalmatia and Northern Italy have been known for some time. However, the most recent comes from Školarke in Slovenia, and this is by far the clearest of the three (*colour plate 4*). It clearly shows a small, possibly circular furnace, with two arched openings. The lower, possibly leading to the hearth, appears to have stylised striated lines inside indicating the fire. The upper arch also shows a curious inverted 'V' feature inside that might represent the crucible. Interestingly, rising out of the top of the furnace are a series of wavy lines imitating heat, suggesting that there was an opening or chimney. To either side of the furnace are sat two figures, one blowing a vessel and another seemingly inspecting a finished one.

Another image of glassmaking comes from a late first or early second-century terracotta group from Egypt (*14*). This depicts Eros stood in front of a glass furnace holding a small bowl-shaped crucible in one hand while with his other hand he is dipping a blowing iron into it. As with the depiction on the lamps, the furnace on the terracotta is probably of the circular variety. Clearly shown is a lower opening at ground level that even appears to project forward somewhat, and an upper opening on top of what appears to be a small working ledge. Above this upper opening, the furnace continues to taper upwards into a tall chimney.

Based upon the archaeological evidence from England and elsewhere, as well as the terracotta lamps, a tentative reconstruction of the circular Roman furnace can be suggested. Sunken slightly below ground level, the fuel is placed in a compartment fed from the front through a projecting firebox. Above this is a ledge, or siege, to hold the crucible at the same level as a gathering hole, where the blowing iron can be inserted.

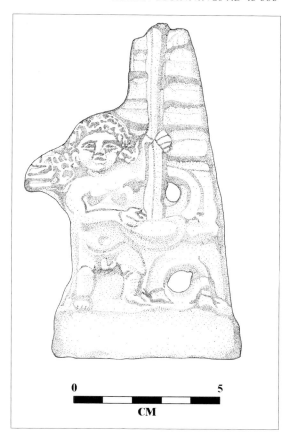

0   5

CM

14 Egyptian terracotta showing Eros at a glass furnace. *After Price*

Finally a tall chimney, necessary to create the draft required to reach the required temperature, tops the superstructure.

While well-excavated furnaces, such as that from Blue Boar Lane, Leicester, are one obvious form of evidence for glassmaking in Roman Britain, glassmaking crucibles are also present on a number of sites where there are no surviving structural remains. Fragments of crucibles containing glass deposits have been found at Silchester, St Albans, Worcester and London. Almost all of these are small bowl-shaped crucibles, although some fragments from London appear to be of the fixed rectangular variety, similar to those from Bonn.

A further indication of glassworking is the presence of glassworking waste associated with blowing. These can be as simple as runs, blobs or small spills, although the most distinctive element of working waste is the moil. Characteristically for the Roman period this takes the form of small circular 'collars' of glass. Ordinarily any waste glass would probably be collected and then remelted, so that any found archaeologically will only represent a tiny proportion of that originally generated. Nevertheless, examples of waste glass and moils are known from Wroxter, Caerleon and Colchester (*15*). However, the largest group thus far found in Roman Britain is over 50kg of waste glass and cullet from the Guildhall Yard, London. Dating to the second century, this area originally lay outside of the fort at Cripplegate next to the amphitheatre and probably represents a group gathered together to be remelted at a furnace somewhere in the near vicinity.

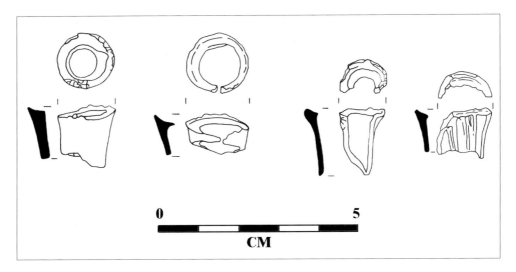

15 Moils found at Sheepen, Colchester. *After Price*

One element that has yet to be found on any site in England is a tool directly associated with glassmaking. This is not surprising; any tools would have been considered valuable and would only have been discarded when broken or rendered unusable. Nevertheless, glassmaking tools found on the Continent suggest what would have been in use in Roman Britain. Perhaps the most impressive set, identified by Jenny Price, came from a fourth to fifth-century context at Mérida in Spain. Among these were fragments of hollow-folded blowing irons and solid pontil rods. Similar tools associated with glassmaking have also been found in Croatia, France and the Ukraine.

PRIMARY AND SECONDARY PRODUCTION REVISITED

The evidence from Britain and other north-western provinces has led to the development of a model of primary production from raw materials on a large scale in the East, followed by the long-distance transport of blocks of glass for secondary remelting and formation into vessels in the West. This model is supported by a significant body of evidence and works if a number of assumptions concerning the nature of the glass industry and its technology are made. The greatest supporting factor for the primary production of all glass in one region is the surprising chemical homogeneity that exists within glasses found across the Western Empire. If glass was being made in a variety of provincial locations from local raw ingredients, a wider range of chemical variations or 'signatures' might be expected. This is certainly true for the medieval and post-medieval periods. Nevertheless, this might not necessarily be the case. Glassmakers of any period make glasses according to recipes that have been developed through experimentation and practice, and perhaps a chemical homogeneity in Roman glasses might be the result of the more universal adoption of 'standard' recipes than occurred in later periods.

While it is clear from evidence such as shipwrecks that a certain amount of raw glass was being shipped as a tradable commodity, it is hard to envisage all glass used in the north-western provinces arriving this way. Although it is difficult to quantify precisely due to the tendency of glass to be recycled, the scale of glass use in Britain alone between the first and fourth centuries would have necessitated a huge level of trade across the Empire in order to satisfy demand. It seems inconceivable that there would have been no attempt to produce glass from raw ingredients closer to the final markets. Even if it is accepted that natron from the Egyptian desert was the sole alkali source used in all Roman glass, there is no reason why this could not be traded and then mixed with local sands and lime to make glass. This, coupled with the relative absence of any firm archaeological evidence for the large-scale primary production dating to between the first and fifth centuries that would have been necessary to supply demand, suggests that an alternative explanation is possible.

Re-inspection of the evidence from Roman Britain and other sites from the north-western provinces suggests that glass could have been, and indeed was, made from raw materials. The most definitive evidence to date comes from the Coppergate excavations at York, where 187 sherds of crucible were found with glass still adhering. Initially thought to date to the ninth century AD, it was subsequently recognised that these were in fact Roman in date, and that they came from just 200m south of the corner of the legionary fortress. The fabric of the crucibles can be identified as Ebor ware, broadly dating them to between AD 71 and 250. Although most of the crucibles only contained fully melted glass, and as such were no different from those found at Silchester or St Albans for example, some contained evidence from primary glass production. This took the form of fragments of partly fused quartz material, or blocks of glass with white frothy layers within it (*colour plate 5*). On visual inspection this appeared to be evidence for the melting of the initial batch of raw ingredients, and this was confirmed scientifically by Caroline Jackson. Chemical analysis (using ICPS) indicated that the composition was similar to the 'standard' composition of natron-based Roman glass. Slightly higher levels of iron and alumina were interpreted as the use of impure sands, while somewhat increased levels of potassium could hint that some plant ash was used in addition to imported natron.

On the basis of this evidence, it is perhaps important that the model of primary and secondary production is re-evaluated. Clearly any conclusion, especially one based on this British evidence alone, can only be tentative. However, it has been demonstrated that at least one episode of primary production occurred at York, and it is likely that it was occurring elsewhere. Certainly it was claimed that, during excavations at Gereonstrasse in Cologne in 1885, and again in 1896, frit as well as blue-green blocks of glass were discovered. Unfortunately this material was dispersed among private collectors and is now lost, so this claim cannot be substantiated. Despite this, evidence for primary production might be seen in the structures of furnaces themselves. It has already been observed at the Eigelstein in Cologne that both rectangular and round furnaces were in operation at the same time. The rectangular furnaces are known to have held large fixed crucibles, quite suitable for fritting and the production of primary glass, while the round furnaces held deeper bowl-shaped crucibles, that were more suited to the dipping and use of blowing irons.

On this evidence it is perhaps possible to suggest that the rectangular furnaces were used for the primary production of glass, which was removed and then melted in the round furnace for secondary working. Although this can only be conjectural, the absence of frit or semi-fused batch material on other sites cannot be taken as evidence for the lack of primary production. Partially fused batch material would only be discarded if something had gone wrong during its production and melting, otherwise it would have been transformed into glass.

To what extend primary production may have been occurring in Roman Britain is less clear, and the predominance of round furnaces might suggest it was limited. However, a rectangular furnace has been found at Caistor and rectangular crucibles at London. Furthermore, the evidence from York suggests that relatively small quantities of glass were being made in ordinary bowl-shaped crucibles, which could indicate that a circular furnace was being used. Whatever the case may be, and even with the very fragmentary evidence, the real possibility remains that glass was being made in Britain from raw ingredients.

THE ROMAN REPERTOIRE

The excavation of most Roman period sites in England will reveal at least some fragments of glass. In common with most periods, it is often hard to attribute a manufacturing provenance to any excavated glass, and this is particularly the case in Roman Britain, given the compositional homogeneity of the glass. Coupled with the relatively ephemeral evidence from production sites, it is virtually impossible to say for certain what vessels and objects were made here; any discussion of the vessels produced must be cautious and primarily concentrate on what it is known was in use, rather than necessarily produced in Britain. Much work in identifying the types of glass found has recently been undertaken, and this has resulted in the most comprehensive publication today, *Romano-British Vessel Glass: A Handbook* by Jennifer Price and Sally Cottam.

Although it is known that some glass was imported into England prior to the Roman invasion, this is extremely rare. With the arrival of the Roman Army in AD 43, glass is found on sites in increasing concentrations. Often these vessels can be closely dated by their archaeological contexts, no more so than at Colchester, or Camulodunum, the first capital of the newly formed province. Excavations from the 1930s onwards have revealed well-stratified sequences of material, including glass, which can be dated to the period between the first foundation of a settlement in AD 43 and its initial destruction during the Boudiccan revolt of AD 60.

Vessels popular during this first-century period include those that were not blown, rather being slumped in an oven to produce the desired shape. The most common of these, the so-called pillar-moulded bowl with its characteristic external ribbing (*16a*), was probably used as a drinking cup rather than a bowl. Other drinking vessels are also found in first-century contexts, including conical-footed beakers and 'Hoffhiem' cups (*16b*). The latter were named after the legionary fortress at Hoffhiem in Germany, where these vessels were first found in numbers. Simple in form with a low pushed-in base and cracked-off rim, these as well as other drinking vessels are often decorated with simple horizontal bands of wheel-cut lines. Clearly such drinking vessels were quick and relatively cheap to produce and it is not surprising that they were relatively common finds on sites.

Other drinking vessels found during this period were those formed by being blown into a multi-piece mould. Normally referred to collectively as 'games cups' due to their decorative themes, they fall into two categories. The first are gladiator cups, where the central element in the decoration consists of fighting gladiators, who are often named above. The second type are circus cups where, instead of gladiators, teams of chariots are shown racing around the circus, represented by spina and other features (*16c*). Although elaborate vessels, games cups made by mould blowing were quick and probably very cheap to produce. They may even have been made as 'souvenir' pieces to be sold at public games and were undoubtedly popular.

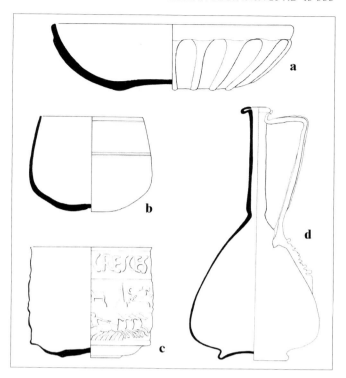

16 Roman glass forms. *After Price & Cottam*

Drinking glasses were not the only wares to be produced in the first and early second centuries; serving vessels such as flasks are also found. These were often tapering in shape, with tall constricted necks, conical bodies and a large angular handle (*16d*). Such flasks could be decorated with blown ribbing and were sometimes made in coloured glasses, with amber, brown and blue being popular. Another form that appeared at the end of the first century was the prismatic bottle. These were thick-walled vessels intended for the storage and transport of either solids or liquids. Although they varied in height from around 15cm to in excess of 40cm, they were usually blown into either a square (*17a*) or hexagonal mould up to the level of their shoulder. Given their shape, prismatic bottles were well suited to being packed into wooden crates for transport, as evidenced by the vertical scratches frequently found on their sides. Although clearly intended for mundane functions, it is not unusual to find prismatic bottles reused as cremation urns, as their relatively wide mouths were suitable for receiving the pieces of burnt bone.

Other containers dating to the first and second centuries were small unguent bottles and bath flasks. The former (*17b*), used to hold perfumes or cosmetic liquids, are frequent finds in burials and on domestic sites alike. Normally long, tapering and with a convex base, these often have evidence for the use of a stopper through the scratches left on the inside of the neck. The bath flask was a slight variation of the small bottle and, although several forms are known, the most common in England was characteristically spherical in shape, with two small loop handles (suitable for suspension) applied to its shoulders. Such flasks were used to carry oil to the baths, and it is not surprising that they are frequently found in their drains and other similar contexts.

The later first and second centuries can be seen as a high point in the use of glass in Roman Britain. It is certainly a period when glass is most commonly found and where

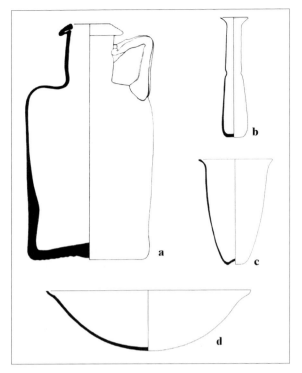

17 Roman glass forms. *After Price & Cottam*

there is the greatest variety of forms. The third century saw the continuation in use of many types, particularly the prismatic bottle and the bath flask.

However, it was during the fourth and fifth centuries that the character of Roman glass in England changed. Not only was the quality of the glass often poorer, with more air bubbles and impurities, there was less attempt to either decolourise or colourise the glass and many vessels had a distinct natural-green tint. The quantities of containers diminished and the prismatic bottle finally went out of use. Glass vessels found were more often than not associated with drinking. Forms typically included tall conical beakers (*17c*), ring-handled flasks and shallow hemispherical bowls (*17d*). A particularly representative assemblage of fourth-century glass was found at Burgh Castle, one of the so-called Saxon shore forts. Also known in England and other north-western provinces are hemispherical bowls with fine engraved scenes, predominantly featuring hunting or biblical motifs. Interestingly, most were engraved with drinking-related slogans such as *Bibe vivas multis annis* (drink, may you live many years).

Not only were vessels a popular glass product, but window glass was also a Roman introduction to England. Window glass is often found on villa sites, and also military sites and towns. Panes of cast window glass were usually small in size, being typically no large than 30-40cm square, although occasionally larger ones are found. Windows made from cylinder glass have also been found on a number of third and fourth-century sites. The resulting window glass is thinner and smoother, but for some reason was never as popular as the cast variety.

Finally, it is important to remember that glass was used for other purposes in Roman Britain. Not only were beads popular, but simple glass bangles and gaming counters were also made. Indeed, many of these did not require the high temperatures needed for vessel production and could have been produced in more localised workshops.

3

A MEDIEVAL CRAFT 500-1500

THE ROMAN TRANSITION

Defining the difference between Roman and Anglo-Saxon glassworking is not as simple as might be thought on first sight. The end of the Roman period in Britain is usually taken as AD 410, the year in which the Emperor Honorius recalled the legions to mainland Europe. While this was also the period that saw the onset of movement and settlement in southern and eastern regions by a number of Germanic groups, the connection between the two events is far from clear cut and, today, archaeologists are more critical of such simplistic divisions. It is clear that Roman Britain did not cease to exist overnight in AD 410 and many urban sites, such as Wroxeter and York, show continuation of occupation well into the fifth century. Furthermore, many rural sites, such as the villa at Barton Court in Berkshire, while apparently in some decline, display evidence for later habitation as well.

Whether Roman industrial traditions continued at this time is unclear as the evidence for early fifth-century glass production and use is scanty at best. Despite the archaeological evidence for glass production in England during the first to third centuries, there is very little for the subsequent century. Perhaps the best evidence is some unpublished fourth-century blowing waste from Binchester, and this has led to the suggestion that glassmaking at this time was restricted to rural areas and thus less likely to be identified archaeologically.

The lack of late Roman production sites is not the only complicating factor in the identification of any continuation of manufacturing traditions. Identifying vessels that may have been used during the crucial two decades either side of the year AD 400 is problematic. This is further complicated by the lack of accurate dating of late Roman sites due to the absence of coins struck between AD 395-403. Despite these chronological problems, some late Roman forms, such as conical beakers with fired round rims and indented hemispherical bowls, continue to be found in fifth-century burials in the South-East of England.

To further complicate matters, England in the early fifth century was not as homogeneous as might be thought. The present-day regions of Cornwall and Devon, as well as large parts of Wales, were never as 'Romanised' as extensively as the rest of the country, so were consequently less affected by the political breakdown of the Roman province. Moreover, these were the same areas that had far less, if any, contact with the fifth-century Germanic migrations. Consequently the earlier medieval period of the fifth to seventh centuries in Britain is often divided between the 'Anglo-Saxon' (northern, central and eastern England) and 'Celtic West' (Scotland, Wales and south-western zones).

EAST AND WEST: THE FIFTH TO SEVENTH CENTURIES

Although a separation into Anglo-Saxon and Celtic West is often visible archaeologically, it is important to remember that these two areas were not entirely separate cultural zones. While there are vessels that are much more common in the so-called Celtic areas, occasional examples of these are found in Anglo-Saxon contexts and vice versa.

Migrating Traditions

Some Roman forms are found in later fifth-century burials in Surrey, Sussex and Kent, suggesting that there was not a complete break with previous traditions of glass use at this time; at least not immediately. However, these vessels are probably the exception, and there is no evidence for a direct continuation of manufacture.

What is apparent is that, during the fifth and early sixth centuries, new ranges of vessels were introduced to eastern England, and Kent in particular. These included the distinctive cone beaker (*18a*) usually decorated with fine trailing and probably imported from northern France or the Low Countries. Likewise, the bell beaker (*18b*) primarily found in Kent, had clear origins in northern France, where it has been identified as a typical Merovingian product. Another characteristic vessel for the period was the claw beaker, with its applied beaks or claws (*18d*), a vessel with a genesis in the fourth-century Rhineland, but which went on to develop during the fifth and sixth centuries across Northern Europe. Many of these shapes, such as the claw and bell beakers, continued

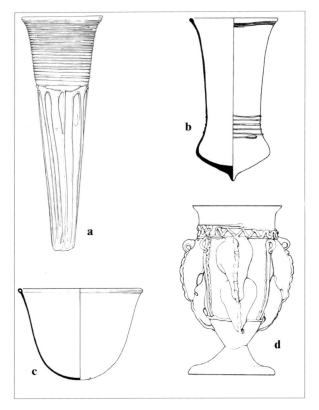

18 Early Saxon vessel forms from the East of England. *After Evison*

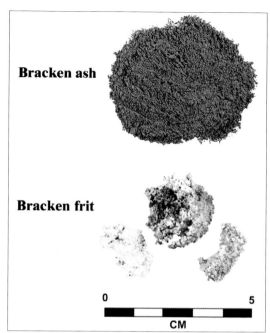

1 Bracken ash, top, and experimental frit made from it, below. *K. Welham, University of Bournemouth*

2 Tombstone of Iulius Alexander. *Museé de la Civilisation gallo-romaine, Lyon*

3 Above The furnace at Blue Boar Lane, Leicester. N.B. scale in feet. *N. Cooper, University of Leicester Archaeological Services*

4 Left Lamp from Školarice, Slovenia, showing a furnace and glassblowers. *I. Lazar, Institute for the Mediterranean Heritage at the University in Koper*

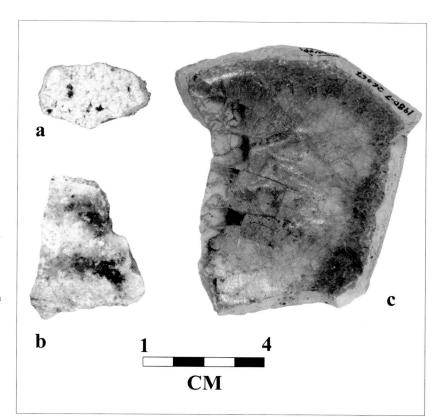

a

b

c

5 *Right* Roman glassmaking waste from Coppergate, York. *C. Jackson, University of Sheffield*

6 *Below* Coloured window glass from Jarrow. *R. Cramp, University of Durham*

1   4

CM

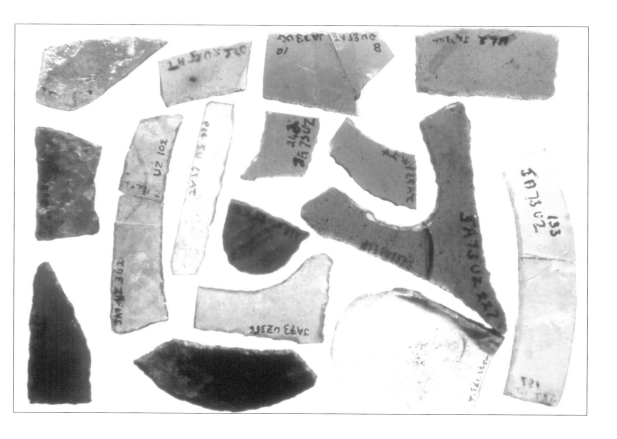

7 The cloister at Glastonbury Abbey, looking north. *Author*

8 Furnace at Barking Abbey. *Newham Museum Service, archive now lodged with Archaeological Data Service, York*

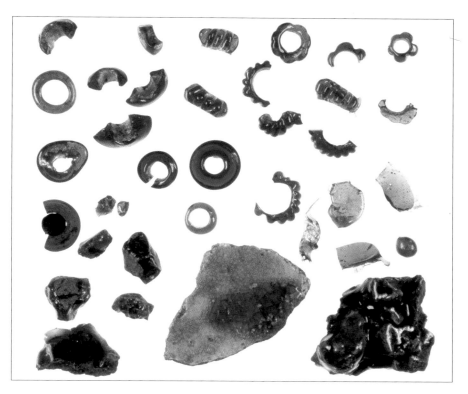

9 Viking bead-making in York. *York Archaeological Trust*

10 A fifteenth-century Italian furnace. *Vatican Library, Chigi F.VIII 188 f.191*

11 Glassmaking at the pit of Memnon, Sir John Mandeville's Travels. *Trustees of the British Library, MS. 24189*

12 The medieval furnace at Little Birches, Wolseley. *D. Crossley*

13 Parody of a doctor and patient from the 'Pilgrimage Window' of York Minster *c.*1325. *Dean and Chapter, York Minster*

14 Annealing oven, furnace four, at Knightons. *D. Crossley*

15 Main furnace at Bagot's Park. *D. Crossley*

16 Furnace one at Little Birches, Wolseley. *D. Crossley*

17 *Above* The furnace at Hutton under excavation. *D. Crossley*

18 *Opposite above* The furnace at Rosedale under excavation. *D. Crossley*

19 *Opposite below* The furnace at Kimmeridge under excavation. *D. Crossley*

in use into the later sixth and seventh centuries, while further forms were introduced. These include the convex-based palm cup (*18c*). Again, it probably developed from Rhenish types and the bag beaker, which has similar parallels in Scandinavia.

Despite this apparent growth in glass use in eastern England, particularly in the context of burial, there is as yet no evidence that it was produced domestically. Indeed, the concentration of vessels in Kent, an area known to have had extensive early trade contacts with the Continent, indicates that all vessels from the fifth to seventh centuries were imported. It has been suggested by Vera Evison that the Kempston-type cone beaker was an early English product due to its almost exclusive distribution in this country. However, until positive evidence for production is found this can only remain speculative.

In spite of the general lack of evidence for fifth to seventh-century production, there are some tentative hints. Eleven crucible sherds were found in a pit at the settlement of Buckden, Cambridgeshire. These contained both yellow and opaque white glass residues and were dated to the sixth century, although these were probably only used for bead manufacture, rather than for producing larger vessels. Other pieces of evidence for actual production during this period come from historical rather than archaeological sources. With the reintroduction of Christianity in the seventh century, there are some early ecclesiastical documents that mention glass production, and window glass in particular. The earliest dates to around AD 669-72, when Bishop Wilfred is said to have glazed St Peter's church in York. What is less clear is whether the glass was manufactured locally or imported. Perhaps firmer evidence can be found in Bede's account of Benedict Biscop's introduction of Gaulish glaziers to provide windows to the monastery of Wearmouth in AD 675. Again, the text is not explicit whether these glaziers made the glass locally or brought it with them. Nevertheless, window glass dating to between the seventh and eleventh centuries has been found on an increasing number of sites in England. Professor Rosemary Cramp has identified seventeen such sites to date, and unsurprisingly twelve of these were ecclesiastical. The largest assemblage, comprising a total of 1,827 fragments, was excavated at Jarrow, the monastery twinned with Wearmouth. This shows that a variety of colours were produced and that highly sophisticated glazing patterns could be achieved (*colour plate 6*).

Celtic Cullet?

Glass has long been found on a number of sites in those western areas not directly influenced by the early Germanic migrations, and as early as 1914 Curle identified early post-Roman fragments at the Mote of Mark in Kirkcudbrightshire. The first possible evidence for production was found during the 1930s at Lagore in Ireland, when the presence of fragments of excavated glass was explained as intentionally gathered cullet for remelting and formation into beads and vessels. However, these were relatively isolated examples, and it was not until the 1950s and the excavation of Dinas Powys in Glamorgan by Leslie Alcock that a substantial assemblage of glass was recovered.

Professor Alcock's excavation of the early medieval settlement produced a large quantity of vessel glass and, at the time, two general observations were made. Firstly, the majority of vessels were cone-shaped beakers, with distinctive opaque white thread trailing (*19*), a form that was rare in eastern parts of England. Secondly, the majority of the assemblage consisted of rim and body sherds, rather than bases, which were thicker and would perhaps be more ordinarily expected to survive. Alcock's interpretation of this peculiarity was that the fragments from Dinas Powys represented collected cullet,

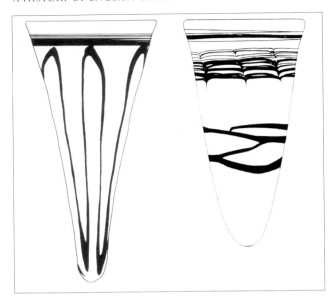

19 Vessel glass forms found in the 'Celtic West'. *After Campbell*

rather than vessels used and broken on site, which was gathered together for melting and reworking. This reasonable assumption seemed to confirm, albeit ephemerally, that early post-Roman manufacture was being undertaken at, or close by, the site.

However, the evidence from Dinas Powys and forty-three other sites has more recently been re-evaluated by Ewan Campbell. His first observation was that the distribution of glass almost exactly mirrored that of imported continental ceramics. While not dismissing the idea that the glass was cullet, it did confirm that there was a real and strong connection between the two. Furthermore, the fragments of glass that did show evidence of melting and heat distortion were distinctly different to the majority of the assemblage. These primarily consisted of deep colours, such as blue and brown, rather than the lighter pale yellow or almost colourless glass that the cone beakers were made in. This led Campbell to suggest that these dark-coloured fragments represent broken glass, or cullet, that was deliberately selected for remelting, possibly as beads or inlays. It therefore indicated that the fragments of cone beakers genuinely did come from vessels used on the site.

This hypothesis was confirmed when Campbell reconstructed the distribution of the cone-beaker fragments, as well as pottery sherds, found in association with Building 2 at Dinas Powys. Fragments originally thought to have come from a number of different cone beakers were demonstrated to actually be portions of the same vessel. Furthermore, it became clear that both the pottery and glass had been broken in the building and their fragments had become subsequently dispersed externally, probably during the course of normal domestic cleaning. This suggested that the majority of glass fragments found at Dinas Powys resulted from use, rather than import as scrap, and seems to diminish the argument for early production, at least on the scale that had once been thought, in the western parts of Britain. The lack of cone-beaker bases now could be explained by the 'nuisance factor'; they were the thickest and most durable parts of the vessel, which were more likely to be picked up and disposed with away from the site, rather than being trampled into the ground. Examination by Campbell of other similar, if smaller, assemblages from Whithorn and Cadbury Congresbury confirmed similar patterns of use and disposal.

The provenance of these fragments, and the distinctive trailed cone beaker in particular, is far from certain. When first excavated on sites earlier last century, it was assumed that they were Germanic or Low Country in origin, so terms such as 'Frankish' or 'Teutonic' were used to describe them. However, the realisation that the opaque white trailed cone beaker was rarely found in these supposed areas of production, particularly those with the characteristic marvered vertical running chevron, has led to the suggestion that they were manufactured elsewhere. The evidence for this, however, has not been so forthcoming. The close correlation in Britain between the occurrence of these cone beakers and pottery known to have been imported from western France has led to the suggestion that the glass might have been produced there as well. The best evidence to confirm this has been found in recent excavations in Bordeaux, where it is clear that glass production was taking place between the fifth and seventh centuries. Furthermore, among the sixth-century forms found at Bordeaux is the cone beaker with similar opaque white trailing to those found in western parts of Britain. If a direct connection can be confirmed through chemical analysis, it would prove that these vessels originated in France.

Despite the lack of evidence for glass production during the sixth and seventh centuries in the Celtic West, a final observation contrasting early glass use here with that in the eastern parts of England can be made. The majority of glass used seems to date to a relatively short chronological period of around AD 500-600. This is at odds with the occurrence of imported ceramics on the same sites, which continue to be found, albeit in diminishing numbers, from well into the eighth century. It would appear that, even though there was clearly access to imported goods during the seventh century and later, the demand for glass was less. This does differ from the picture in eastern areas of England, where the demand for glass continued to increase during the Middle Saxon period.

LATER SAXON PRODUCTION: THE EIGHTH TO EARLY ELEVENTH CENTURIES

The evidence for glass production in both eastern and western parts of the country is poor at best for the fifth to seventh centuries. What limited proof there is, in the form of some melted cullet in western areas and the crucibles from Buckden, suggests that any manufacture was on a very small scale, probably limited to the making of beads and coloured inlays. However, from the eighth century onwards there is increasing evidence for larger-scale manufacture in England, very possibly from primary ingredients.

Glastonbury

The best-known and, until recently, the most comprehensive evidence for glassmaking in mid and later Saxon England was found during the 1950s by Raleigh Radford at Glastonbury Abbey. Excavating in the cloister area of the thirteenth-century abbey, he found the remains of the earlier Saxon monastery (*colour plate 7*). Furthermore, he encountered evidence for some of the industrial complex that accompanied the institution, and these included signs of glassworking and what appeared to be four actual furnaces. However, before this evidence is discussed, it is important to add a slight note of caution, as the site was never properly published, and Raleigh Radford seems to have left much of the actual investigation of the furnaces to Donald Harden, a noted art historian, but by no means an accomplished field archaeologist. Justine Bayley has recently brought together the records from the excavation and subsequent work undertaken by Harden, although much of the original evidence is now missing or is more poorly recorded than might be hoped for. Furthermore, although professional for its time, the excavation techniques employed do not match those of today, and knowledge of ancient glassmaking techniques was far less advanced. For example, Raleigh Radford's definition of a furnace was merely a depression or hole associated with working waste, as opposed to a definable structure. Nevertheless, it is possible to reconstruct the appearance of at least some of the structures and suggest what they might have produced.

Although found in the cloister of the thirteenth-century abbey, Raleigh Radford's work had already shown that the Saxon church lay further to the north-west, and the furnaces were located in a subsidiary craft-working area. Although four furnaces were identified, only two survived sufficiently to indicate their actual form. The illustrated plans of both of these, known to have been properly drawn at the time, are now lost and all we can rely on are measured sketches from the site notebooks, which Bayley has reproduced. The first and best-preserved furnace was found in 1955, being oval and approximately 1.2m x 0.9m in diameter (20). Only the base survived as a hollow, but this incorporated reused Roman tile to form an efficient refractory layer. The very lower part of the furnace superstructure was around the edge of this lined hollow and it indicated that the walls were made from clay, baked hard by the heat. At the western end of the furnace, on its narrowest axis, was an apparent opening, probably for stoking the furnace. Covering the floor Radford found 'many small scraps of glass, the largest barely one inch square, and pieces of crucibles with glaze adhering'.

The second relatively well-preserved furnace was located by Raleigh Radford in 1956 and excavated the following year by Harden. Again this was oval in shape but larger, being approximately 2m x 1.20m (21). As with the other furnace, only the base survived and this consisted of yellow clay with burnt mortar and charcoal flecks pressed in, overlain by at least two layers of burnt material, presumably deriving from the last firing of the furnace. Unlike the other structure, the opening of the stoke hole was on its longer axis, and there was tentative evidence for a firebox in front of this. Virtually no glass was recovered from

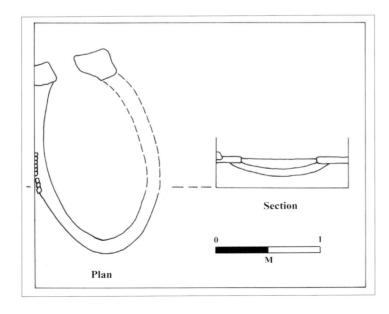

Section

0   1

M

Plan

20 Glastonbury furnace one. *After Bayley*

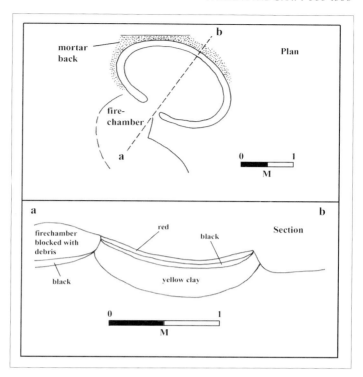

21 Glastonbury furnace
two. *After Bayley*

this furnace, but Harden did identify lumps of baked clay, which probably came from the lost superstructure. Evidence for two other furnaces was also found in 1956 and 1957, but these were either too poorly preserved or recorded to add further to our knowledge of the physical structure of a later Saxon furnace. They did, however, provide more fragments of glass waste, crucibles and other secondary production evidence.

While these excavations provide interesting evidence for melting ovens, they do provoke as many questions as they answer. The first concerns the nature of the products being manufactured on site. About twenty-nine fragments of crucible (half that originally found) survived for study today. All contained residues of glass and this appeared to be almost exclusively blue/green in colour. Furthermore, other working waste, such as lumps, drips and even moils were all blue/green. However, the fragments identified as possible products were not so homogeneous and both window and vessel glass were found. The majority of the window glass was the same blue/green colour as the waste material and glasses in the crucibles, suggesting that it was a possible product. The vessel glass was less uniform, with pieces of olive, green/brown and colourless vessels recovered. This might possibly indicate that the vessel glass was imported cullet, brought on site for remelting and the production of window glass.

The second, and more problematic, question that arises is the actual date of the furnaces themselves. At the time of excavation Radford and Harden thought them to date to the ninth or tenth centuries. In 1957 Robert Cook took a series of samples from the burnt base of the second furnace in what was a very early attempt to establish an archaeomagnetic date. Unfortunately, both contemporary and subsequent reanalysis of his data has produced results that are far too scattered to be meaningful, as they span the whole of the Roman and Saxon periods.

Perhaps the most interesting dating evidence has been provided by Vera Evison's study of the vessel glass found at the site. It must be emphasised that only twenty-two fragments now survive, far too small a group to provide definitive results. However, among the vessel glass only two forms could be identified: the palm cup, or funnel beaker, and the globular beaker, both common mid-Saxon forms. If it is assumed that these vessels represent products, they give a date for production somewhere during the later seventh or eighth centuries. On the other hand, it seems possible that these vessel fragments were actually collected cullet. Consequently, they only provide a *terminus ad quem* to the late seventh century, and the furnaces could indeed have been considerably later if they were using old cullet. However, if this was the case and they belonged to the ninth or tenth century, it would seem strange that the cullet was so uniformly earlier in date and that no later vessel types were found among it. Therefore, due to the limited evidence, the age of the excavation and the subsequent loss of many of the finds, the precise dating of the Glastonbury furnaces can only be tentatively postulated, but somewhere in the late eighth or early ninth centuries would not be unreasonable.

Other Later Production Evidence

While Glastonbury remains the 'type-site' for Saxon glassworking in England, there is a reasonable amount of more recent archaeological evidence that should not be overshadowed by it. In particular, a well-preserved Saxon furnace has been found at Barking Abbey, Essex, although this still awaits full publication. In 1990, excavations revealed the first comprehensive remains for such a structure since those at Glastonbury over forty years earlier. Being a recent excavation, the level of recording provides a clearer picture of Saxon glassmaking during this period. Only one oven was found, although this lay on top of an area of heavy burning that might itself have been an earlier demolished furnace. The structure was slightly more circular in shape and was approximately 2m in diameter (*colour plate 8*). The base was formed from baked clay that, like one of the Glastonbury furnaces, was inset in its surface with reused Roman tiles. The clay sides survived around the edge of this base to a height of 20cm.

As well as the furnace resembling those found at Glastonbury, a series of pits clearly associated with the structure provided further evidence for glassworking. In these were found the remains of a tile and fired-clay 'tank' similar to examples known on a number of Roman sites and used as a crucible to melt glass. Also in the pits were pieces of furnace superstructure, and even a broken *tuyère*, showing that a bellows was used to force air into the furnace. What has generated most interest, however, are the fragments of glass and working waste. These included sections of reticello or polychrome glass rods, formed on site by twisting together canes of glass of different colours. At this stage it is uncertain what was being manufactured at the site, but the presence of the reticello rods suggests that vessels were among its repertoire. No evidence was found for production from primary materials, but this does not necessarily indicate that this did not occur on site, and the large tank crucible would seem to suggest that glass was being melted, if not made, in quite considerable quantities.

As with the furnaces from Glastonbury, the dating of the Barking evidence has been the focus of debate. Some have suggested a mid-Saxon date, due to the similarity of some of the working waste to that at Glastonbury. However, this is tenuous at best and archaeomagnetic dating of the soil beneath the surviving furnace has produced a date of 925 ± 50, and the other burnt area thought to be an earlier furnace a date of 920

± 50. In the face of such strong scientific evidence, a late ninth or early tenth century date must be accepted, and it is extremely unlikely that the glass in the associated pits somehow relates to an earlier phase of glassmaking.

Other evidence for later manufacture survives at other sites. The most complex and perhaps controversial is the 'Viking' furnace found during the Coppergate excavations in York. In searching for archaeological evidence of York's Scandinavian past, the not-inconsiderable amount of glassworking evidence found on the site was initially assumed to be Viking. Much of this is now known to be in fact Roman, although the structure identified as a furnace does have an archaeomagnetic date of around 860 AD. However, it is far from certain that it was even used for producing glass, its square-tiled shape could have been used for a variety of purposes and the site stratigraphy is such that it is hard to be certain whether the melted blobs of glass found in association with it derive from the same phase of activity. More convincing evidence for later glassworking has been found elsewhere in York (discussed below).

Ephemeral evidence comes from finds of tenth and eleventh-century crucibles in Lincoln and Gloucester. At Lincoln twenty-one crucibles containing green or yellow glass were recovered, as well as what was interpreted by Justine Bayley as a block of cullet. These finds come from a relatively closely dated context of around 970-1010 AD. The tenth-century finds from Gloucester include a similar number of crucible fragments with yellowish glass on their surfaces. Interestingly, both these glasses proved on analysis to be very high in lead oxide, a type of glass known to have been particularly favoured for the manufacture of beads.

Other evidence for glassworking, and vessel manufacture in particular, has come from recent excavations by English Heritage at Whitby Abbey. Glass fragments and at least one twisted reticello rod have been found in contexts dating to the eighth or ninth centuries. It is likely that future excavations will reveal an increasing number of crucibles, working waste and maybe even furnaces from the mid-late Saxon periods.

It is important to remember, however, that not all glass manufacture required complex furnace structures or even crucibles. Bead manufacture in particular could leave very scanty remains that are less likely to survive archaeologically. Perhaps the best example of this can be seen at 22 Piccadilly, York. Here, a number of early eleventh-century contexts contained evidence of bead manufacture (*colour plate 9*). This took the form of small discs cut or broken from Stamford ware sherds. On these, collected Roman blue glass was melted and beads formed by scraping and rolling. All stages of this process were found on the site, from the ceramic discs and melted cullet to malformed beads and finished products. A similar 'pallet', this time made from fired clay, was found at Gloucester, and other Stamford ware sherds associated with bead-making have also been found at Coppergate, York.

THE SAXO–NORMAN TRANSITION: THE LATER ELEVENTH AND TWELFTH CENTURIES

Despite the evidence from the later Saxon period, it appears that there was a cessation in glass production during the early to mid-eleventh century, and there is little evidence for glass use in England during the late eleventh and twelfth centuries. Only very occasional fragments of vessel glass are found archaeologically, and the few surviving examples of window glass from this period were almost certainly imported.

It is perhaps tempting to see this decline in production and use as somehow related to the Norman Invasion. However, the evidence for glass use in the decades prior to the invasion is increasingly scarce. Although glass is still very occasionally found on mid-eleventh-century sites, such as window glass dating to the 1050s from Edward the Confessor's new Westminster Cathedral, there is no evidence it was produced there. Consequently the decline in glass production must be seen as predating the Normans, a situation that merely continued after the invasion. This is contrary to what might be expected for window glass, given the enormous ecclesiastical programmes embarked upon immediately after the conquest. Although it would appear that early castles had few windows that might require glazing, the newly introduced Romanesque style incorporated much large window openings than the late Saxon church builders had. While other substances, such as horn, waxed cloth or even simple wooden shutters, could have been used to cover these windows, it is likely that many were glazed. This is confirmed by evidence from several sites, such as York Minster, where eleventh or early twelfth-century window glass has been found archaeologically. However, the reglazing and rebuilding programmes of the later medieval and post-medieval periods have destroyed most of this evidence.

Why vessel glass seems to be absent during this period is also unclear and less easy to explain. Unfortunately, as yet, there has been insufficient study of the evidence for glass production and use in eleventh and twelfth-century Normandy, so it is not possible to contrast any differing patterns between there and England. As a consequence it is not possible to directly equate the apparent cessation of production in England to any domestic political changes. However, there is a more direct correlation between the waning of the appearance of glass and the nature of the material itself.

It has long been recognised that there is a distinct difference between the glass found in England in the later Saxon period and that produced from the twelfth century onwards. The earlier glass is typically a soda-based metal and, although the source for this was not the same imported natron used in Roman glass, seaweeds were almost certainly burnt to produce a soda ash. By contrast, during the eleventh century it is apparent from the rare pieces of glass sometimes found that a new type of potash glass was being produced, at least in Northern Europe. This appeared to use burnt wood or bracken ashes, which contained much higher levels of potassium and produced a more discoloured glass, usually with a heavy green tint.

The reason for this transition from soda to potash glasses is unclear. It is unlikely that the soda-rich plants burnt in the ninth century suddenly ceased to be available in the eleventh. The most likely explanation is that, with an apparent cessation of domestic production in England, probably during the late tenth century, any glass required had to be imported from abroad. While Saxon glassmakers, with England's extensive coastlines, had no problems with access to soda-rich plants for their ash, those areas now supplying England might not have been so fortunate. This would seem to indicate that there was a switch of supply. Whereas, prior to the tenth century, glass might either have been produced at home or imported from other coastal zones, such as Scandinavia or northern Germany, later it was being supplied from areas further from the sea on the mainland. Therefore, it might be argued that the switch from soda to potash glass represents a strengthening and developing of longer-distance trade routes, rather than a retrograde step, as is sometimes assumed.

TWO TRADITIONS: THE THIRTEENTH TO FIFTEENTH CENTURIES

Despite the virtual absence of information on glass manufacture during the tenth and twelfth centuries, from the thirteenth century onwards there is much better evidence for both production and use in England. During this period it is important to look too at the wider European industry, as the later Middle Ages was a time of increasing international exchange; not only of goods, but also technological expertise and even craftsmen.

Conventionally the glass industry of later medieval Europe is divided into two traditions, the 'Southern' and 'Northern'. However, this dichotomy is simplistic, particularly when the Mediterranean world is considered. With the steady growth of the Byzantine Empire out of the former eastern provinces of the Roman Empire, there were clearly areas of Europe that suffered fewer disruptions to everyday life, which in turn may have affected their techniques of glass production. Even in Italy, southern France and Spain, western provinces subject to 'barbarian' incursions, it is clear that the Roman way of life continued and developed largely uninterrupted. Unfortunately, the true nature and extent of the Byzantine glass industry is unclear: few vessels or objects of definitive Byzantine provenance have been identified.

Rather more is known about the emerging Islamic traditions. With the expansion of the early Caliphates of Egypt, Palestine, Syria and Iran into areas previously controlled by the Byzantine or Sassanian Empires, an emergent Islamic industry becomes apparent. The earliest evidence comes from Raqqa in Syria, where furnaces of eighth to ninth-century origin have been found, while later documentary sources indicate that Tyre and Antioch in the twelfth century, Aleppo in the thirteenth century and Damascus in the fourteenth century were all centres of production. With the growth of large-scale and sophisticated Islamic industries, it was inevitable that this would influence neighbouring European production.

The 'Southern Tradition'

Discussion of the southern European tradition of glassmaking is inevitably linked with Venice, and it is often assumed that the Venetians were the earliest practitioners of an increasingly sophisticated medieval industry. However, this has tended to mask the importance of other glassmaking centres elsewhere in Italy, southern France and subsequently Spain. It is true that the first named Venetian glassmaker can be found in a deed as early as 982, more than 100 years before the next recorded individual, a Robert Vitrearius at the French abbey at Maillezais. However, the creation of the Venetian supremacy 'myth' was only cemented in the thirteenth century, when the Venetian state became increasingly protectionist of its industry. This finally resulted, in 1292, in the wholesale movement of all the glassmakers to the island of Murano, where they were banned from leaving without permission.

It is perhaps ironic that, given the historical scale of the Venetian industry, very little is actually known archaeologically about the methods of production. Vessels made there can be identified across Europe, and some glass and waste has been recovered from the lagoon. However, not a single furnace site has been properly excavated, mainly due to the fact that their locations are still used for the production of glass today, so remain inaccessible or have been completely destroyed by subsequent redevelopment.

However, recent years have seen the identification, survey and excavation of medieval glassmaking sites elsewhere, and Tuscany in particular. These help outline the style of southern production and indicate whether it had a wider effect on the situation in northern Europe and England in particular. The site of Monte Lecco, Liguria, was excavated in 1956, and the ground plan of a relatively well-preserved furnace was found (*22*). What was revealed was a circular structure around 3m in diameter externally. The furnace floor was flagged and there was not a well-defined flue but, instead, and in similar fashion to the earlier Roman circular furnace, there was a square sunken firebox that fed into the furnace base. The walls, built of bonded stone, rose to a maximum height of 45cm and there is evidence in at least part of the structure for a shelf, or siege, for the crucibles to sit on. Unfortunately the remains of the superstructure were missing. Apart from this circular feature, and associated working areas and waste, there was little further evidence for the superstructure of the furnace or how it might have been worked. This circular form is mirrored at other excavated Italian sites, such as Val d'Elsa, although again

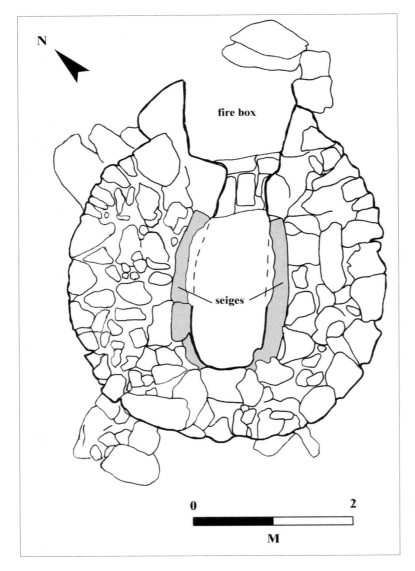

22 Medieval furnace from Monte Lecco, Italy. *After Fossati & Mannoni*

the archaeological remains are not particularly helpful in reconstructing the original appearance of the furnace and other sources of information need to be considered.

Perhaps the clearest of these can be found in Agricola's *De Re Metallica*, published in 1556. Although a sixteenth-century treatise that described the production of glass, among other crafts, it reflects the development of an earlier tradition. Furthermore, the contemporary woodcut illustrations illustrate a circular domed furnace that would have been completely familiar to the thirteenth-century glassmaker (*23*). Similar to the excavated evidence, Agricola's furnace has a flat fire chamber at floor level without a flue, fed from a single stoke hole. Above this, and partially open to it, was the working or melting chamber where a number of crucibles sat on a continuously running siege, with each being accessible from an individual gathering hole. Finally, above, and connected to this, is a small chamber in the top of the furnace, which is usually interpreted as an annealing oven.

23 A circular furnace depicted in Agricola's *De Re Metallica* of 1556.

This probable layout of the furnace is interesting for a number of reasons. For instance, it does suggest that many of the glassmaking processes from melting to annealing might have been undertaken in a single structure. Also, it is important to speculate how draught control might have been achieved; with both the excavated and illustrated examples there is no indication of the presence of a flue to direct air into the furnace, and it seems that the stoking and gathering holes served this purpose. Furthermore, Agricola's illustration depicts a furnace with a completely covered domed roof, without any means of channelling the air upwards. This is usually the accepted form for such a furnace, but there are other possibilities. For example, a unique *maiolica* model of an Italian furnace has survived and is now preserved in the Science Museum, London (*24*). Although eighteenth-century in date, it still appears to resemble the medieval form, but in this case the model clearly has a small chimney visible on the top of the dome. This would certainly aid airflow through the furnace, but might make using the upper chamber as an annealing oven more problematic as it would certainly have increased the heat in this area considerably. Perhaps if a chimney was used then a separate annealing oven would be required, and interestingly the *maiolica* model clearly shows a second rectangular feature attached to the main furnace, which could have been used for this purpose. Whatever the case might be, it is clear a number of possibilities are possible.

The 'Northern Tradition'

As already observed, the so-called 'northern tradition', of later medieval glassmaking is typified by two distinct differences when compared to areas south of the Alps. The first is that, at some point during the tenth and eleventh centuries, there was a shift in the type of flux used, away from the soda-rich alkalis imported from the Mediterranean or made from marine plants, towards the use of forest-derived plant ash, usually assumed to be either bracken, beech or birch.

24 Italian Maiolica model of a furnace. *Science Museum, London*

The second difference between the traditions of north and south are the designs of the furnaces used to produce the glass. While the circular furnace dominated the southern industry, it appears that a rectangular design was used in the north. This is in part confirmed archaeologically. The emphasis on the rectangular furnace in previous scholarship is largely due to a single, if remarkable source, Theophilus' *De Diversis Artibus*. This book of thirty-one chapters is devoted to glassmaking and was compiled by the Benedictine monk Roger de Helmarshausen between 1110-40. In it he gave a detailed description of how to construct the main melting furnace 'of stones and clay, 15 feet long and ten feet wide' as well as 'another furnace ten feet long, eight feet wide and four feet high' for annealing. It is clear from his text that Theophilus had experienced glassmaking at first hand, and his account is not disputed. However, as a single source it has rather lead to the assumption that all medieval furnaces of this and later dates would broadly follow the same form. While this was probably the case, to date there have not been sufficient numbers of excavated examples to tell for certain.

The Documented Industry in England

Just as there is a lack of archaeological evidence for glass production prior to the thirteenth century in England, the same is equally true for the historical record. A single exception is an oblique reference in Norfolk to a 'Henry Daniel vitriarius' during the course of the reign of Stephen (1135-54). The description of the man as 'vitriarius' or 'glassman' is interesting, as it is an epithet often used in the later medieval period. However, its interpretation must be treated with some caution. While it might indeed refer to a producer of glass, glaziers or even traders might also be so labelled.

The earliest and most frequently quoted reference attributable to a glassmaker occurs in the thirteenth century. At some time immediately prior to 1240 (the document is not dated, but must have been drawn before this date) a grant of 20 acres of land near Chiddingfold in Surrey was made to 'Laurence Vitrearius'. This lease of such a sizable area of woodland would suggest its intended use for fuel, and possible raw material, for glassmaking. How long this enterprise lasted is uncertain, but Laurence's son William le Verir appears to have taken over the business.

Chiddingfold was at the heart of the Surrey-Sussex Weald, an area immensely important for several medieval industries due to the large area of woodland that was carefully managed for this purpose. Consequently, it is not surprising that frequent references to glassmaking occur in the area, and these were comprehensively drawn together by Kenyon in his *Glass Industry of the Weald*, published in 1967. In 1351 John Alemayne (the German) was paid 43s 6d for 87 weys (approximately 435lbs or 200kg) of white glass and William Homere a further 8s 8d to carry it from Chiddingfold to the Royal Palace at Windsor, where it was used for glazing the chapel. It is interesting to note that as much as a sixth of the total cost of the glass was spent on its transport, indicating that this was a laborious task that had to be undertaken with care, and emphasising that the relatively close proximity of glassmaking areas to their principal markets was crucial. Other similar payments can be found at this time. John Alemayne was paid to supply 400lbs of glass to Windsor again in 1355, and John Brampton in 1378 for 120lbs of Wealden glass for the King's palace at Woodstock.

Records also survive that do not directly relate to or name glassmakers in the Weald and elsewhere, but do shed further light on the medieval industry. By 1328 there was a registered London guild of glaziers, and members of this guild are recorded as searching for good sources of high-quality window glass. For example, in 1351 John Geddyng, the third upper warden in the guild, was recorded as looking for glass in the Wealden region, while another firm of agents, Dedington & Son, actually had a headquarters at Chiddingfold and, at various points during the later fourteenth century, supplied window glass to Merton, Winchester and New Colleges.

Despite its relatively close proximity to London, the Weald is not the only area for which documentation concerning the glass industry survives, nor did these areas have to lie so close to the capital. In 1349 John Brampton, the glazier, already noted to have purchased glass in the Weald in 1378, also bought glass from unnamed sources in Shropshire and Staffordshire for St Stephen's chapel at Westminster. Staffordshire is again mentioned as a glass-producing area when, in 1380, John Glasewryth moved from there to lease half the glasshouse at Kirdford, Sussex from the widow of John Schurterre.

Indeed, it is apparent that, outside the Weald, south-east Staffordshire was one of the largest glassmaking centres. In this area two close concentrations of glassmaking were indicated in the documents, situated either side of the river Trent. The first was centred just to the north of the village of Abbots Bromley, in part of what later became Bagot's Park. As early as 1289 'le glasslone' (glass lane) is mentioned in the area, and a number of glassmakers are recorded as living in Abbots Bromley; in 1327 there was a Richard and Thomas le Glasmon and later in 1332 a Simon le Glasmon. The second area referred to in the contemporary documentation was just south of the Trent to the west of the village of Rugeley, although records only start in the fifteenth century. In 1447 there was single reference to 'Glashoushey', whereas during the 1470s there were more concrete indications of an established industry. In November 1478 the rent of 'le glashows' was listed as 7l 6s 8d and the next year 5s was charged for the sale of fern to the glasshouse. A possible individual related to this operation can also be identified, for in 1479 a Thomas Wakelen was described as a glassmaker of Ruggeley. References also exist for other areas of England: for example the fourteenth and fifteenth-century pipe rolls for Cumbria record a number of times 'le glashous' in Inglewood Forest and even name John Vitriarius in 1317.

The Wealden industry is also documented during the fourteenth, fifteenth and early sixteenth centuries, although there are gaps in the sources. One family that rose to prominence during the fourteenth century were the Schurterres. The first member documented as being directly involved with glassmaking in 1367 was John Schurterre, who died in 1379. At least two further generations of this family were mentioned as continuing on the family business during the fourteenth century. Indeed, the Schurterres are mentioned in parish records until the early sixteenth century, although none are directly mentioned as glassmakers after around 1400.

It is not possible to identify individual glassmakers or their families in the Weald during the course of the fifteenth and early sixteenth centuries, and it is only through inference that the gap can be filled. One family that may have been working at this time were the Peytowes. The first firm record of their involvement with the industry is the will of John Petowe, dated 4 April 1536, where he bequeathed to his son John '10s of suche things as shall come and be made of the glasshowse and all my toyles and moulds as belongeth to the glasshowse'. However, despite this late date the Peytowes were recorded as having lived at the same location in Chiddingfold since the 1440s when John's grandfather Thomas purchased the property, and it is possible that they had earlier undocumented interests in the glass industry. Certainly the site continued to be used for glass production until John's grandson, also called John, died in 1613.

Whether based in the Weald, Staffordshire or elsewhere, what is of particular interest is that, in all these cases, the documented industry was located in heavily wooded areas, presumably due to the need for large quantities of fuel for the production process. The only exceptions to this were occasional, and short-lived, glasshouses associated with specific building programmes or commissions. One of the earliest of these was operating between 1284-1309 at the Abbey of Vale Royal, Cheshire, specifically to supply window glass for the foundation. Likewise, during the fifteenth century the 'glashous' at Salisbury Cathedral is recorded to have ordered batches of sand, suggesting that manufacture, as well as the preparation of glazing, was being undertaken on site.

The final documentary sources that shed light on the medieval industry in England were pictorial representations of glassmakers and glassmaking. A number of well-known depictions survive in manuscripts produced in Southern Europe. The earliest of these can be found in the text of *De Universo* by Rabanus Maurus, dating to 1023, and housed in the library at Monte Casino. Although highly stylised, it appears to show a three-tiered structure, with a firebox at the base, a series of gathering holes above and then an annealing chamber at the top. However, despite being marred by the lack of artistic perspective, it would appear that the structure is circular in plan, and thus an early example of the 'southern' style furnace. Later-medieval depictions of circular southern furnaces are also known. The clearest is from a late fifteenth-century manuscript in the Vatican library (*colour plate 10*). Again, the structure was three-tiered, having a square opening to the fire chamber, a series of gathering holes below which sits a working ledge, and then a small annealing chamber in the top. It would seem that these images are accurate depictions of the type of furnace in use in the Mediterranean world, and they certainly conform to later post-medieval designs, their relevance limited in aiding reconstruction of those used in England.

There is, however, a manuscript that has caused considerable discussion concerning the form of the northern furnace, and is often taken to represent a typical forest furnace. Now housed in the British Library, an illuminated copy of *Sir John Mandeville's Travels* contains a scene of glassmaking at the Pit of Memnon. This document, thought to have been executed in Bohemia in around 1410, is incredibly detailed (*colour plate 11*). Kenyon discussed this image in connection with his research on the Wealden furnaces of southern England. He interpreted it as a rectangular structure, perhaps with slightly rounded corners, and equated it with the physical remains of English medieval furnaces. This has more or less been the subsequent interpretation of this structure. A note of slight caution was sounded by Robert Charleston, who looked at the evidence for excavated furnaces in Bohemia, which all had oval ground plans. As a consequence, he suggests the Mandeville structure was oval rather than rectangular, but still essentially 'northern' in character, with its long fire trench running the whole length of the structure.

However, closer inspection of the manuscript perhaps reveals a different interpretation. The right-hand portion of the furnace appears to be much more circular in plan, and the left-hand side appears to be a distinct, if attached, feature. If this is so, the best interpretation might be that it is actually a circular furnace and, instead of having an annealing chamber above it, has a separate structure for this purpose. If this is indeed a correct reading of the illustration it is rather removed from the rectangular furnace described by Theophilus and assumed to be the norm for Northern Europe at this time. Interestingly, this plan of a circular furnace and attached oven is rather reminiscent of later post-medieval furnaces on mainland Europe, such as the recently excavated Soop furnace in Amsterdam, dated to the first decade of the seventeenth century. What is perhaps more important about the Mandeville illumination is the setting that the glasshouse is placed in. It is clearly in a wooded environment and, at the top of the picture, the raw materials of glassmaking are shown being gathered up. The glasshouse is depicted as being covered by a rather temporary or ephemeral structure, and the actions of the glassmakers are very realistic, suggesting that the illustrator had witnessed glassmaking at first hand.

ARCHAEOLOGICAL RESEARCH ON THE MEDIEVAL INDUSTRY

While the documented history can identify areas and individuals involved with glassmaking in medieval England, it is less informative concerning the actual practices undertaken, or the precise forms of furnaces employed. However, the last century has seen a growing interest and research into the surviving archaeological remains of the industry.

The Surrey-Sussex Weald

As has already been noted, the Wealden area of Surrey and Sussex has long been identified as the major centre of glassmaking in medieval England. Documents mention the names of glassmakers and the parishes in which they lived and died. It was through the course of early research into this documentation that the first archaeological investigations were initiated. The pioneer of this approach in the Weald was the Reverend T.S. Cooper. While ministering to the parish, he started to prepare a detailed, yet never published, history of Chiddingfold, which he soon discovered had a rich history of glassmaking; so much so that he dedicated a whole chapter to the topic. Discovering that glassmaking had taken place in the parish made him and his family search for sites. Between 1911 and Cooper's death in 1918 they had discovered and investigated four sites, three of which were probably medieval in date. Scant notes that survive show that his family (at this stage he was too ill himself) uncovered portions of these furnaces and collected a considerable amount of glass, now deposited in Guildford and Haslemere museums. Unfortunately, the records of these excavations (if they ever existed) do not survive.

Cooper's work was followed by that of S.E. Winbolt, a local schoolteacher, between the 1920s and early 1940s. An enthusiastic amateur archaeologist, Winbolt was keen to extend the search for sites beyond just the parish of Chiddingfold. He undertook frequent excavations, some of which he recorded with reasonable accuracy; others less so. Of these excavations, some proved to be medieval in date, such as at Hazelbridge Hanger, and the material he collected was important to later studies. In 1933 his rather hastily produced *Wealden Glass: The Surrey-Sussex Glass Industry* was published, incorporating many of his findings. After its publication he continued to be active in researching the Wealden industry until his death in 1944.

But perhaps Winbolt's true legacy was slightly more indirect, for it was a frequent helper on his excavations, Kenyon, who was to make the greatest and longest-lasting impact on the archaeological study of the Wealden industry. Over twenty years after Winbolt's death Kenyon sought to collate all the information gathered and not properly published by Cooper and Winbolt, as well as add any new evidence that had come to light. In *The Glass Industry of the Weald* he was able to assemble a schedule of forty-two known or probable glassmaking sites in the Weald (*25*). These were identified, classified and broadly dated through excavation, place-name evidence, chance finds and associated pottery finds. As a result, Kenyon could identify fourteen sites (*26*) that could be classed as 'early' or before 1550. Unfortunately, in a reassessment of these sites in 1991-93 by

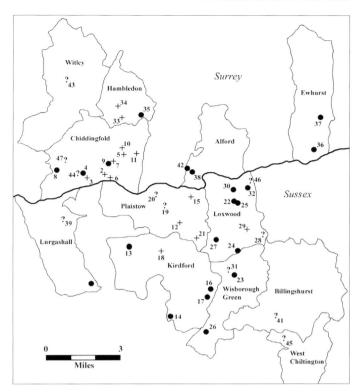

Right: 25 Location of glassmaking sites in the Weald. *Adapted from Crossley*

Below: 26 Table of 'early' glassmaking sites in the Weald. *Adapted from Kenyon*

No	Name	Window glass	Vessels glass
2	Gostrode I	crown	yes but unspecified
3	Upper Chaleshurst	crown & broad	yes but unspecified
5	Fromes Copse	yes but unspecified	flasks, lamps, urinals?
6	Gostrode II	uncertain	uncertain
7	Hazelbridge Hanger	uncertain	uncertain
10	Prestwick Manor	uncertain	uncertain
11	Redwood	uncertain	flasks?
12	Crouchland	yes but unspecified	yes but unspecified
15	Hogwood	uncertain	uncertain
18	Little Slifehurst	yes but unspecified	yes but unspecified
21	Wephurst Copse	crown	lamps
29	Malham Ashford	broad (inc. ruby glass)	uncertain
33	Blunden's Wood	yes but unspecified	flasks, lamps
34	Gunter's Wood	crown	lamps

David Crossley, three were shown to be subsequently destroyed and a further three could no longer be traced.

The form of these early phase Wealden furnaces is unfortunately rather more obscure. Two were excavated by Winbolt and revisited by Kenyon. At Malham Ashford (no. twenty-nine), Winbolt recorded three phases of activity, but no plans survive. At Hazelbridge Hanger (no. seven) Winbolt records a rectangular furnace 4.5m x 3m and a separate rectangular annealing chamber, all set within a boundary ditch. But his plan is so schematic as to be useless in understanding how the site functioned, although continued survival of earthworks suggest that re-excavation would provide a valuable clarification of this plan (27). Interestingly, he did record finding large quantities of waste glass at Malham Ashford, including lumps coloured opaque red, again confirmed by Kenyon.

It is therefore unfortunate that, in an area with such historical documentation, so little firm archaeological evidence has been brought to light, despite its obvious potential. However, there is one site that has produced more concrete results, although the quality of the excavation recording leaves something to be desired. The site, Blunden's Wood, was discovered by accident in 1959 three-quarters of a mile south-east of Hambleton. When first found it took the form of two mounds, the first 4.8m across and 0.6m high, the second being slightly smaller at 3m in diameter. The area was subsequently excavated by Eric Wood very rapidly over three weekends in 1960.

On clearance the different mounds appeared to cover two distinct areas of glassmaking activity (28). The larger eastern mound occupied the location of the main melting oven, furnace A. This was a rectangular structure 3.3m x 3m, built around a long central clay-lined flue approximately 0.6m in diameter, although this was subsequently choked by molten glass and waste, probably the reason for the furnace's abandonment. Either side of the flue were two sieges, constructed from sandstone blocks. These were 2.4m long, 0.65m wide and, where they survived sufficiently to be measured, 0.6m high. Interestingly the southern siege, which was much better preserved than the northern one that had collapsed,

27 The furnace area at Hazelbridge Hanger. *D. Crossley*

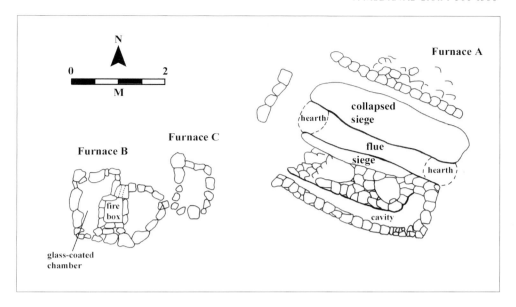

28 Plan of furnaces at Blunden's Wood. *After Wood*

had two circular depressions 38cm wide where the crucibles would have sat. Beyond the sieges lay the outer sandstone wall base of the furnace, but separated by a slight gap filled with clay. This wall only survived up to the height of the siege, and the form of the roof is unknown. The function of this gap is less certain, but Wood interpreted it as an insulation cavity. Finally, at either end of the flue, patches of burning indicated that two hearths were set to provide the heat, and the low remains of the 'screening wall' to shield workers from the heat was found at the eastern end of the flue. Although the excavation plan is difficult to make out, Wood did produce a reconstruction drawing that, on current evidence, still remains a probable and accurate impression of the furnace when it was in use (*29*).

The second mound produced more ephemeral remains on excavation, and these are not so easy to reconstruct and interpret. The central feature was the irregular-shaped furnace B, which measured 2.4m x 1.35m (*28*). It had a central clay-lined firebox, with evidence for heavy burning and even a *tuyère* for the insertion of a bellows. Either side was a chamber, the western of which had the remains of splashed glass on its walls. Interestingly, this second structure also produced the largest quantity of glass and crucible fragments in its fill. A final structure, furnace C, lay between the two other furnaces and was formed by an oval of large stones, 0.75m x 0.45m, surrounding a patch of blackened soil.

Some of these features are rather difficult to interpret. The main furnace A was clearly for melting glass and held four pots at any one time. Wood interpreted the second irregular furnace B as having the dual functions of fritting on the left-hand side and annealing on the right. However, this does not fit with the evidence. Fritting would not have produced splashes of glass on one side of the oven, and the presence of a *tuyère* indicated the need to force a draft, suggesting that higher temperatures were required than those need for either fritting or annealing. Certainly, the presence of molten glass on the structure suggests that melting was taking place here. Finally, Wood interpreted the oval structure, furnace C, as being for preheating and firing the crucibles, known as

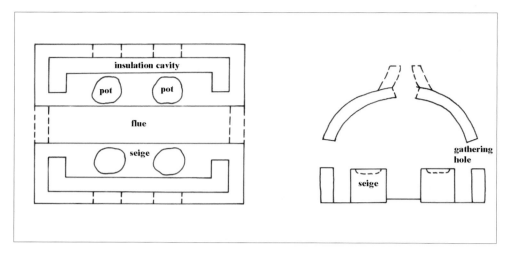

29 Reconstruction of the main furnace at Blunden's Wood. *After Wood*

potarching, and while this may be true there is no evidence either way to support it and it would seem a little small for this purpose.

As with the excavation of most furnace sites, there were many finds associated with the structures. Most numerous were fragments of crucibles, and two broad medieval types can be identified (*30*). The first was bucket-shaped, being about 35cm high and with near vertical sides, and with a rim with a diameter also of around 35cm. The second, more numerous type, was more convex-sided, or barrel-shaped. They were slightly smaller, being around 30cm tall, and had out-turned rims of about 25-30cm diameter. Other finds were scarcer; the only glassworking tool found was part of a common type of shovel, which was probably used to feed the hearths. A large quantity of glass waste was recovered, as were some fragments of typical medieval green glass. Examination of this suggested that both vessels and windows were produced at the site (discussed further below).

Another point of interest concerning the Blunden's Wood furnace is its precise date. Prior to its discovery in 1959, there were only a few vague hints in Winbolt's *Wealden Glass* that a furnace might be present in this location. There was, however, no indication of its age. Once excavated, sixteen samples were taken from the furnace for archaeo-magnetic dating. This now-established technique is not an unproblematic one even today. In 1960 it was entirely innovative and it provided a date of last firing for the furnace of around 1330, a figure that is repeated unquestioned in all the subsequent literature. However, this result was reached through comparison of the data with only two other sites of known date. While it is fairly certain Blunden's Wood is a medieval furnace, a date of 1330 cannot be treated as absolute. A small assemblage of pottery was also found at the site, the most distinctive fabric being Cheam ware. Normally this pottery is dated to the second half of the fourteenth century, suggesting that the furnace too might be slightly later than first thought. Unfortunately, however, Wood does not report whether the ceramics were found in primary contexts associated with the furnace's construction and use, or in layers formed following its abandonment.

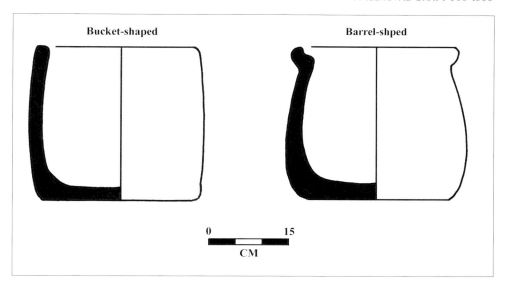

30 Crucibles from Blunden's Wood. *After Wood*

Staffordshire

As already noted, documentary sources suggest that medieval glassmaking concentrated in two areas of south-east Staffordshire, which were very close together. Archaeological evidence for this has been less forthcoming. While post-medieval glassmaking in the area was explored in the 1960s, it was not until the 1990s that any evidence for medieval furnaces were found. None of these lie within the area of Abbots Bromley, despite the suggestion in the surviving documents that glassmaking was going on there from the thirteenth century. Just to the north-east of the small village of Colton, which lies between the two suggested zones of manufacture, glassmaking waste and crucibles of a medieval type were found at Lount Farm, although without any evidence of an actual furnace structure.

The remaining archaeological evidence comes from the east of Rugeley in the area of the Wolseley estate. At Cattail Pool, an area that has suffered heavy cultivation for nearly two centuries, spreads of dark soil containing crucible and glass waste were identified as the remains of totally ploughed-out furnaces. Although some of the glass and crucible is clearly post-medieval, other fragments appear to be medieval in date. Indeed, research by Christopher Welsh suggests that one of the ploughed-out medieval furnaces at Cattail Pool is probably the site for which the rental payment of 7*l* 6*s* 8*d* was made in 1478.

However, the best archaeological evidence for glassmaking at Wolseley comes from a site just to the west of Cattail Pool at Little Birches. Accidentally discovered in 1990, the area was excavated by Walsh in 1991-92. Two phases of glassmaking were revealed (*31*), the best preserved of which were furnaces 1-3 and lay to the south of the site, although they dated to the first half of the sixteenth century (discussed in chapter four). However, to the north of the site was an earlier phase, which contained furnace 4. The remains of this furnace were quite slight, it having been demolished almost to ground level (*32*, *colour plate 12*). However, what survived was an irregular central flue 2.6m long and 0.45-0.5m wide. Either side were the battered remains of the sieges made from sandstone, and the faint remains of a possible outer wall. Together this indicates that the original width of the furnace was approximately 2m. Furnace 4 was surrounded to the west and south

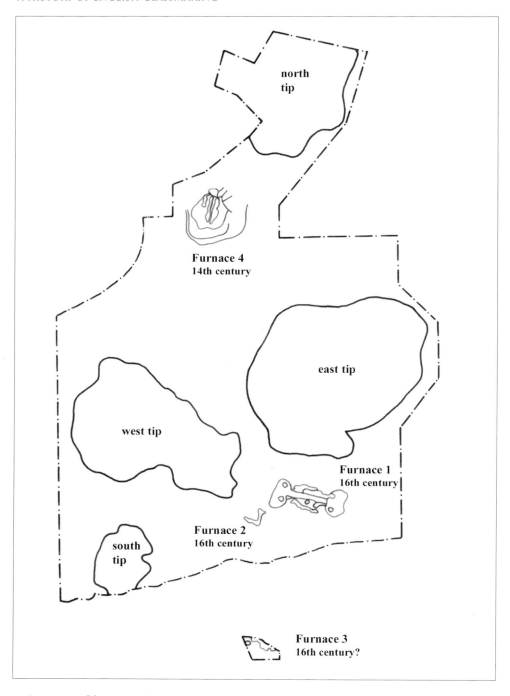

north tip

Furnace 4
14th century

east tip

west tip

Furnace 1
16th century

Furnace 2
16th century

south tip

Furnace 3
16th century?

31 Locations of furnaces at Wolseley, Staffordshire. *After Walsh*

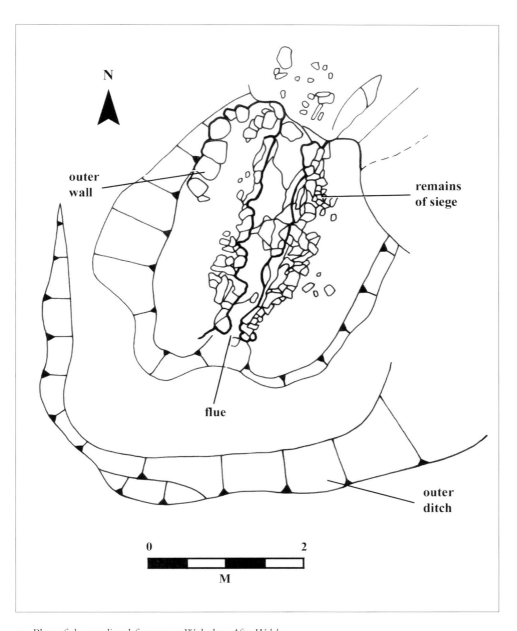

N

outer
wall

remains
of siege

flue

outer
ditch

0   2

M

32 Plan of the medieval furnace at Wolseley. *After Walsh*

by a shallow gully, either to divert the movement of groundwater or, more likely, to act as drainage for a now undetectable lightweight roofing structure.

Associated with the furnace were a relatively large number of pieces of crucible. Although heavily fragmented, they were either bucket or barrel-shaped, like the examples from Blunden's Wood, and had an average rim diameter of 28cm. Unfortunately only nine fragments of glass were recovered and these were heavily weathered. Furthermore, assigning a precise date to the furnace is problematic. It was too disturbed for an archaeomagnetic date to be ascertained, and radiocarbon dating was not undertaken (had it been it is unlikely it would have produced a useful date). However, ceramics found in direct association with furnace features suggest that it was operating at some point during the thirteenth or fourteenth centuries.

There is one site in Cheshire, also worthy of a brief note, that has been partially investigated. It is located at a spot known as Glaziers' Hollow in the Kingswood division of Delamere Forest. Its location is interesting, as this is very close to the Vale Royal Abbey, already noted to have had its own glass furnace in operation between 1284-1309. Whether this particular site was included in the Forest Liberties of the abbey is unknown, and the abbey's own records include another reference to a glasshouse in this area. In 1346/7 a complaint was made against Warren le Grosvenour for encroaching on the abbey's lands at 'le Huvyng and the whole wood towards the glassworks next Heytelegh'. Unfortunately, neither of these two place names can be accurately pinpointed today. Excavations first in 1935, and then in 1947, opened a series of narrow slit trenches over the area so to avoid damaging the tree plantation then occupying the site. A burnt furnace floor was found, as well as a large quantity of glassworking debris and domestic pottery dating to the fourteenth and fifteenth centuries. The debris included fragments of medieval barrel-shaped crucibles with out-turned rims (33), and evidence through discarded moils for the production of plain and coloured crown glass for glazing. No evidence for vessel glass manufacture was found. Whether this site can be definitely linked to the Abbey of Vale Royal or not, it still remains the only archaeological evidence for medieval manufacture in Cheshire.

Further Archaeological Considerations

Despite a century of archaeological work on the medieval glass industry, it is perhaps surprising that only two furnaces have, to date, been properly excavated. Furthermore, both are rather unsatisfactory in illustrating the nature of the medieval industry; Blunden's Wood due to its poor recording, and Little Birches due to its heavy disturbance. Neither furnace can be firmly dated, although it seems likely that Blunden's Wood dates to the thirteenth century and Little Birches to the thirteenth or fourteenth century. Consequently any conclusions concerning the structures used and the technology employed must be fairly general, and treated cautiously until further excavation can take place.

The two main furnaces at these sites do broadly conform to the description given by Theophilus, especially that at Blunden's Wood, although Little Birches is somewhat shorter and narrower. The subsidiary structures of furnaces at Blunden's Wood are harder to interpret, but it seems rather less likely that they were used for fritting and annealing, as originally suggested. One aspect of design poorly understood at both these sites is the precise form of the superstructure. Theophilus suggests a barrel-vaulted roof was required, and this would seem the most logical design from a structural point of view. Wood thought that the roof of Blunden's Wood might have been made from a blend of stone and clay, but acknowledged that this would be difficult to construct.

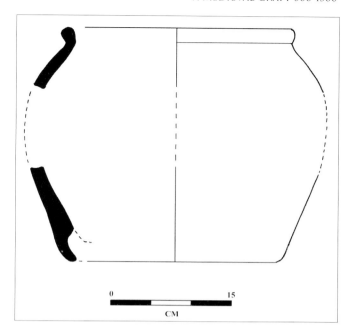

33 Crucible fragments from
Delamere Forest, Cheshire.
After Newstead

0   15
CM

However, in any discussion of medieval glassmaking there is one site that, although early seventeenth century in date, should be considered. In the small village of Shinrone, County Offaly in the Republic of Ireland, is quite possibly one of the most remarkable survivals of a glass furnace from any period. Its ground plan is instantly familiar (*34*), having a central flue and siege benches either side of about 2m in length and with scars that show they originally supported two crucibles each. The outer wall is about 0.3m thick and at the northern end of the flue is a patch of burnt clay, suggesting the location of at least one hearth. The similarity to Blunden's Wood is immediately apparent; however, what Shinrone possesses is its near-complete superstructure (*35*). Built in sandstone, the outer walls rise vertically to the level of the gathering holes and the spring into a rounded vault. The whole of the inside of these walls are splashed with glass. What are missing are the end walls, and it seems likely that they were built more ephemerally, possibly from clay, so that they could be removed from time to time to allow the changing of crucibles and general maintenance to occur. It is not inconceivable that medieval furnaces in England had a very similar appearance.

THE OUTPUT OF THE FURNACES

Given the limited amount of evidence available, when assessing the likely products of the medieval industry in England, any conclusions must be treated with caution. The historical documentation is rarely specific about the output of the furnaces. Furthermore, the archaeological evidence, where it exists, is potentially misleading. It can reasonably be assumed that not all the glass found at a site will have been produced there; the collection of cullet for remelting was a standard practice in most periods. Consequently it is often only through careful examination of the material that some suggestions can be made.

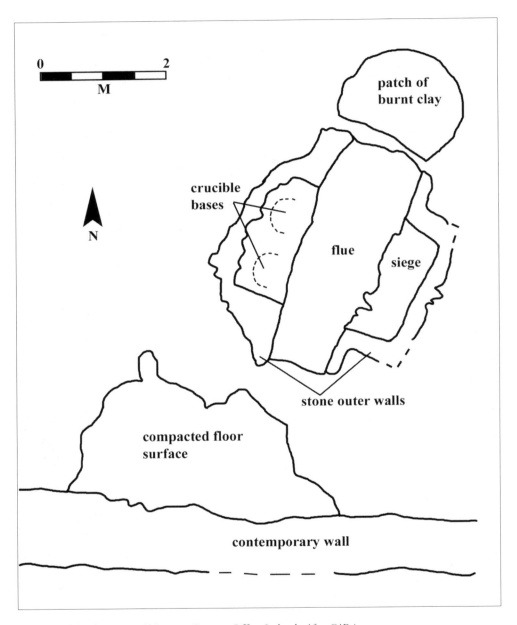

34 Plan of the furnace at Shinrone, County Offlay, Ireland. *After O'Brien*

35 The superstructure of the furnace at Shinrone. *C. O'Brien, Duchas*

Perhaps one of the products easiest to identify from the contemporary documentation is window glass. The orders already outlined for glass from both the Weald and Staffordshire make it clear that this was probably their primary product. Likewise, furnaces established for specific projects, such as at Salisbury Cathedral, would have been exclusively for the production of panes for glazing. However, what the documents often do not say is whether the glass was made using the crown or cylinder glass methods. It is often stated that, in the medieval period, most window glass was made by the crown technique, with broad glass becoming more popular in the sixteenth century, possibly as a result of immigrant glassworkers. However, this temporal division is incorrect and both crown and broad glass was used in medieval England.

Less clear is the extent of vessel manufacture, and there are only rare documentary references to the practice at all. Most notable was one that occurs in the indenture drawn up by Joan Schurtere when she brought John Glasewryth from Staffordshire to help run her furnace in April 1380. It is stated that she undertook to pay him 'for a sheu of brodeglas, 20d and for a hundred of vessel, 6d for his labour'. The exact quantity of window glass that a 'sheu' represented is unknown, but it is interesting that it specifically refers to broad glass. Unfortunately, there is no hint as to what the vessels might be, but these were clearly being produced in some numbers, if John was being paid by the hundred.

The archaeological evidence, almost exclusively from the Weald, also confirms this picture of mixed manufacture at furnace sites. Based on Kenyon's own work and his re-evaluation of Cooper and Winbolt's collections, it is possible to identify potential products from ten of the fourteen suggested medieval sites. In most cases there appears to have been window and vessel production occurring simultaneously. Evidence for broad and crown glass was found and, uniquely, at Malham Ashford, there was even evidence for the working of red glass, possibly for coloured windows. However, this is an exception, and all other Wealden glass, whether used for windows or vessels, is a typical potash-based glass, which had a usually dark-green tint to it.

It is more difficult to identify vessel forms, as most of the material came from surface collections and might be products or collected cullet. However, standard potash glass forms, such as flasks and lamps, reoccur frequently. There is even mention by Winbolt of 'bottles with wide flat lips… some with flute necks, swelling out of a pear-shaped body' at Fromes Copse, a description that may well be that of a urinal. The only properly excavated assemblage of glass from the Weald at Blunden's Wood conforms to this picture, there being flask necks and bases as well as lamp bases (36).

It is unfortunate that, at present, comparable data is not available for other areas of the country, although it is probable that the range of vessel produced was similar. The final way to assess what was produced is to briefly examine the vessels known to have been used in domestic contexts in England. While it is obvious that not all medieval glass found archaeologically in England would have been produced here, it is possible to make some suggestions. From the thirteenth century onwards glass that was clearly imported can be identified in contexts associated with elite groups. Clear glass beakers, sometimes with elaborate enamelling, or tall-stemmed goblets are known as typical forms of the period. However, these elaborate tablewares are usually made in high-quality soda-based or occasionally even high-lead glass, which differs from the typical potash-based metal found at English production sites. It is clear that these tablewares must be imported vessels, and parallels can be found in Italy and southern France, among other places, suggesting their manufacture there.

Nonetheless, the glass most commonly found in medieval England is a potash type, and those vessels usually include flasks and hanging lamps. The former was probably

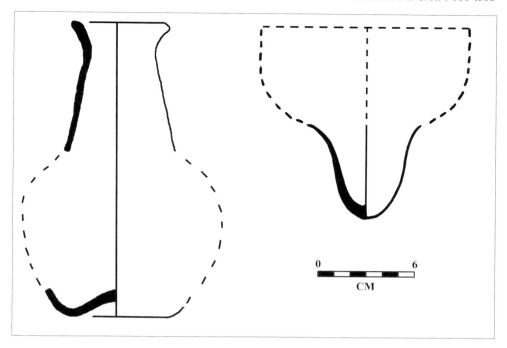

Above: *36* Products from Blunden's Wood. *After Wood*

Right: *37* A late medieval urinal. *Author*

used to hold a wide variety of liquids both on and off the table. The latter seems to have been largely restricted to churches and high-status secular environments, but lamps, with their floating wicks, were an important method of internal illumination. One type of vessel often found in domestic contexts but apparently under-represented on English glassmaking sites is the urinal. These had a spherical body blown to extreme thinness to allow the unobscured observation of the urine's colour for the purpose of health divination. This was such a common medical health practice that not only were finds of urinals relatively common on medieval sites (*37*), they were often used for parodied depictions of the medical profession (*colour plate 13*). Perhaps the reason that urinals have not been recognised by earlier research in the Weald is the nature of their design. Their rims and necks resemble those of a flask while their bodies, being so thin, are unlikely to survive. Their most distinctive feature, their convex bases, probably were confused with those from lamps.

It must be recognised that the evidence for the output of the English medieval industry is limited. The majority of the glass produced was almost certainly for glazing either ecclesiastical or high-status secular buildings. But early glassmakers were also willing to supply what vessel glass they could when there was a demand for it. Although the green potash glass they produced restricted them to more utilitarian forms such as flasks, lamps and urinals, there was apparently still a wide market for these products.

4

IMMIGRANTS AND ENTREPRENEURS 1500-1650

AN ENGLISH CRAFT IN DECLINE

For the first half of the sixteenth century there is relatively little historical evidence for glassmaking in England. This is perhaps surprising, given the numbers of records that survive for the previous three centuries, and the increasing amount of administrative documentation that was being generated in Tudor England. It is possible that this might just be an historical aberration, but it would appear to reflect a situation on the ground where far less production genuinely appears to have been undertaken. Contemporary commentators confirm this picture. For example, the poet Charnock, in his *Breviary of Philosophy*, published in 1557, included the verses:

As for the glassmakers, they be scant in the land,
but one there is as I do understand
and in Sussex is his habitacion,
at Chiddingfold he works of his occupacion.

To go to him it is necessary and meete,
or sende a servante that is discreete,
and desire him in most humble wise,
to blow thee a glass after thy devise.

It were worth many an Arme or Legge,
he could shape it to an Egge,
to open and close as a haire,
if thou have such a one thou needest not fear.

Whether these sentiments are wholly accurate is uncertain, it is interesting to note that, in his slightly indignant tone, Charnock suggests that due to the scarcity of glassmakers this unnamed individual could afford to be arrogant and charge an 'arme and a legge'. Furthermore this reference to Chiddingfold as a centre of glassmaking confirms that medieval glassmaking traditions in the region had continued into the sixteenth century.

Despite this, there are references to only three families operating in the Weald in the first half of the sixteenth century. The first were the Peytowes who, as discussed earlier, can be seen to have been involved in the industry, and resident at Chiddingfold, from at least the 1440s. The first reference to them in the sixteenth century was in the will of John Peytowe who, in 1536, bequeathed to his son John all his tools and moulds as well as 10s of the glass produced at his glasshouse. There was another branch of the same family operating in the Weald at this time, but they were apparently based at Combe, as in April 1563 the will of Thomas Peytowe left his only son William 'his tools, woodstuff and other things belonging to his glasshouse'. It would seem that William continued in the family business, and Thomas's grandson John was later described as a glassmaker in the parish register for 1613. Furthermore, in 1580 there was also a Stephen Peyto described as a glassmaker in the neighbouring parish of Witley, although his exact connection with the main family is uncertain.

Another family associated with the sixteenth-century industry were the Strudwicks. Like the Peytowes they had been resident in the Weald since the fifteenth century, being based in the parish of Kirdford. However, the first mention of them as glassmakers came in 1557 when Henry Strudwyke left to his sons Richard and William 'the profit of my Glasse House with all the beches that I have bought and halfe the beches in and uppon Idehurst and Croftes aforesaid'. He further stipulated that, when Robert reached the age of twenty-two, the two brothers were to divide between them 'all and every suche implements, as is ther occupied, as ovyns, irons and other thinges necessarye to ye said Glasse Howse belonginge'. Later on, at least three other Strudwicks described as glassmakers appeared as witnesses in the Chichester Consistency Court between 1575-86, while as late as 1614 a Henry Strudwick was described as a 'glassscarryer'.

Only one other family was mentioned by name in relation to the glass industry at this time, and this was confined to a single reference. In 1547 Richard Mose, 'glassmaker', bought land at Kirdford and Plaistow, although it is not known whether he actually produced glass there and, if he did, for how long. The limited number of families associated with the Wealden industry at this time was also commented upon in later documentation. In a petition made in 1621 it was stated that 'the families namely Strodwicks and Petoes' were the only ones left working immediately prior to the 1560s.

For areas outside of the Weald there is even less documentary evidence for glassmaking during the first half of the sixteenth century. One exception is south-eastern Staffordshire, where it was noted in chapter three that there was an established medieval industry centred around two locations at Abbots Bromley and Wolseley near Rugeley. While it is probable that glassmaking close to both these villages continued into the sixteenth century, the only surviving documentary sources centre on Abbots Bromley. The first of these was a charter dated 1501, where John Harvey of Queche granted a croft to Thomas Harvey, 'glassmaker', of Abbots Bromley. This land subsequently passed through Thomas's family, who continued to be associated with the glass industry. A John Harvey, glassmaker, witnessed a deed in 1530 and another Thomas Harvey, also a glassmaker, paid a rent of 30s and 'unam fen' (a window), for his holding at Abbots Bromley in 1543. Other glassmakers from different families were also mentioned in the village. In 1517, Ralph Cowper, 'glassmaker', was witness to a deed, and both George Watkys and Thomas Rodes were described as 'vitriarius' in the burial register of Abbots Bromley church in 1566 and 1587 respectively.

Despite the named presence of a few families in both the Weald and Staffordshire, it is clear that the first half of the sixteenth century saw a genuine decline in all levels of production. This would appear to have affected not only the numbers of glassmakers operating, but also their repertoire. It has been suggested by Eleanor Godfrey that, by the mid-sixteenth century, production of window glass had ceased and only vessels continued to be made. Whether this is absolutely true is uncertain, as the reference to Thomas Harvey supplying a window as rent in 1534 would suggest he was also making the glass.

However, it does seem that there was a genuine trend away from window-glass production. By 1567 an unnamed master of a glasshouse at Chiddingfold (so possibly a Peytowe) claimed that he could not make window glass, only 'small things like urinals, bottles and other small wares'. Likewise, in the already mentioned petition of 1621, it was stated that, in the period prior to the 1560s, the Peytowes and Strudwicks only practiced 'the Art of making drinking glasses' and that at the time 'the Art of making window glass was lost in this Kingdom'.

The reason for the decline in window manufacture, which had once been the mainstay of the medieval industry, is somewhat of a mystery. Godfrey suggested that there was no longer a market for glass from ecclesiastical sources, particularly with the Reformation. However, this argument is far from certain as, presumably, the iconoclasm that accompanied the Reformation would have created a sudden demand for new, albeit plain, windows for the majority of churches that survived. Likewise, the sixteenth century was increasingly a time where new secular building projects required greater amounts of window glass. Having noted this, Godfrey rightly pointed out that, alongside a slump in the domestic window glass industry, there was also a decrease in its importation. Her examination of the 1567 Port Books show that windows made up just less than half the glass brought into the country.

ARCHAEOLOGICAL EVIDENCE FROM THE TRANSITIONAL PERIOD

Whatever the cause of the decline of window-glass manufacture, the archaeological evidence for this period is equally scarce. In Kenyon's examination of all known Weald sites, he was unable to positively date any to the first half of the sixteenth century. Four he hesitantly classed as 'transitional' (38), due to the occurrence of fragments of glass that did not fit into his clear divisions of early and later glassmaking sites, and it is possible that these date to this period. Likewise, at least some of the twelve Wealden sites of unknown date might belong to this group (39). However, until further fieldwork and excavation is undertaken, this must remain speculative.

No.	Name	Parish	Condition 1991-93
13	Frithfold Copse	Kirdford	Surviving
16	Indehurst Copse N.	Kirdford	Surviving
17	Indehurst Copse S.	Kirdford	Surviving
42	Knightons	Alfold	Excavated

38 Table of 'transitional' glassmaking sites in the Weald. *Adapted from Kenyon*

No.	Name	Parish	Condition 1991-93
1	Bowbrooks	Chiddingfold	Unknown
19	Lyons Farm	Plaistow	Unknown
20	Shortlands Copse	Plaistow	Destroyed
28	Malham Farm	Loxwood	Surviving
31	Sparr Farm	Wisborough Green	Unknown
39	Lower Roundhurst	Lurgashall	Surviving
41	Lordings Farm	Billingshurst	Surviving
43	Mare Hill	Witley	Surviving
44	June Hill	Chiddingfold	Destroyed
45	Steepwood Farm	West Chiltington	Surviving
46	Primrose Copse	Loxwood	Surviving
47	Frillinghurst	Chiddingfold	Surviving

39 Table of glassmaking sites of unknown date in the Weald. *Adapted from Kenyon*

One Wealden site that does date to the first half of the sixteenth century and has been excavated is Knightons. The site itself was unrecorded until its accidental discovery in 1965. Lying on the parish boundary of Alford and Dunsford, Surrey, it happened to be in very close proximity to another already known furnace at Sidney Wood. Soon after the site's discovery, a series of excavations were undertaken between 1965-73 by Eric Wood and the Surrey Archaeology Society.

At least two phases of activity were observed but, unfortunately, the standard of recording was poor: resulting plans are highly schematic (*40*). Despite this, it is still possible to see a number of important features. Several structures were uncovered and they appeared to have performed a variety of functions. Probably the earliest of these was furnace 1, rectangular in shape and measuring 4.5m x 3.2m. The two parallel siege benches were made from stones roughly packed in clay and there was evidence that they would have held three crucibles each. Interestingly, the fire trench that ran between them, and was 0.76m wide, only appears to have had a hearth at the eastern end, as opposed to one at either end as might be expected.

The whole of this first furnace structure was later deliberately dismantled and replaced, and partly overlapped, by a second, slightly smaller, rectangular furnace measuring 4.3 x 2.8m, again holding three crucibles on each siege. Immediately to the south of these two furnaces was apparently a third one but, from the published records, its precise form and function is uncertain (*41*). In the schematic plan it is shown as another six-pot melting furnace (no. three), albeit attached to another ill-defined structure. However, in the brief description of its excavation Wood claimed to have found 'frit', and therefore suggested it was a fritting oven. However, there is little evidence for this and in all likelihood the 'frit' was merely scum or gall scraped from the crucible, making this third furnace just another rectangular melting oven.

Perhaps the most interesting feature was furnace 4, lying slightly to the west of the others. It took the form of two small square chambers, 1.9m x 1.2m and 2.2m x 1.5m, joined together by a small flue (*colour plate 14*). Both the floors of these chambers were reddened from burning, but clean of ash or slag. Finds from within them included bottle necks, bases and quite a thick layer made up from fragments of crown glass, as well a 1550 shilling of Edward VII. Wood interpreted this feature as an annealing oven, specifically for large crowns of window glass. This is still a plausible explanation, although quite how the square chambers were heated remains uncertain.

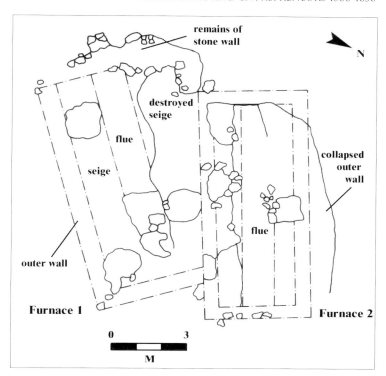

40 Melting furnaces 1 and 2, at Knightons. *After Wood*

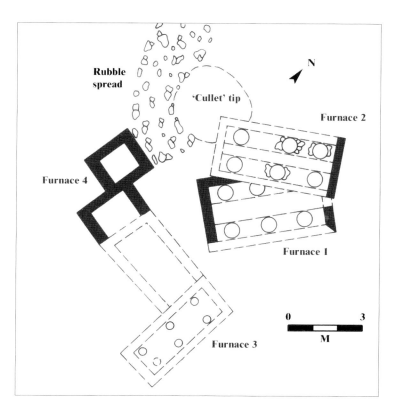

41 Other features at Knightons. *After Wood*

The final important feature on the site was a large 'cullet' dump observed to the west of the furnaces and up to 15cm thick. Although he only partially sampled it, Wood suggested this contained 61kgs of glass. What this glass might represent is slightly problematic. It could be cullet collected from a wide area, or be the result of waste produced on the site, or most likely a mixture of the two. It certainly contained evidence for the production of crown glass, but numerous fragments of pedestal beakers, cylindrical beakers, wrythen flasks, sand glasses and urinals were present. Other finds included significant quantities of crucible fragments, mainly of the bucket-shaped variety, but also some rims from more convex-sided barrel types. The final find of interest was a small section of tubular metal, possibly from a blowing iron.

Knightons is a very interesting furnace for several reasons. The firm date suggested by the 1550 coin of Edward VII was confirmed by an archaeomagnetic sample. Furthermore, the vessel glass found is all typologically from the earlier, rather than the later, sixteenth century. This places Knightons into the period of 'transitional'-style furnaces and not the 'later' period as Kenyon first thought, although the site was not fully published when he wrote *The Glass Industry of the Weald*. As such, it remains the only excavated example that can be said to follow an essentially medieval form in the post-medieval period, and at a time when glass production seems to have been very depressed.

With the exception of Knightons, the lack of archaeological evidence for glasshouses dating to the first half of the sixteenth century in the Weald is largely mirrored in other areas of the country. The only exception is in south-east Staffordshire at Bagot's Park, near Abbots Bromley, an area noted to have surviving records for glassmaking at this time. During large-scale drainage and clearance of part of the park in 1965 as part of a programme of land reclamation for arable farming, fifteen different furnace sites were identified and their locations recorded. Most were heavily disturbed and subsequently destroyed by this clearance. Their exact dates were uncertain but, from the glass finds and associated ceramics, at least some would seem to date to the early sixteenth century.

One of the sites seemed better preserved and a significant quantity of glass was noted, leading to its selection for full excavation in the summer of 1966 by David Crossley. A large rectangular area next to the Storey Brook was stripped and two furnace structures identified (42). The first, to the north-east, was the better preserved and was clearly a main melting furnace (colour plate 15). On clearance, its main features were a pair of stone-built sieges about 80cm wide, and with a stone flue extension at the north-east end and a similar, but brick-built, one to the south-west end. On either siege platform it was possible to see from patterns in the spilt glass that each had originally held three crucibles with base diameters of between 30-36cm.

The flue floor was lined with flat stones but choked with a thick deposit of glass waste. At either end of the flue were patches of highly burnt clay and ash, indicating the locations of the hearths used to heat the structure. Interestingly, analysis of charcoal samples from these hearths indicated that alder was the wood most frequently burnt, although other species were present. About 1.5m from either end of the flues were pairs of large postholes, with the large stone packing still in place. These were to hold upright posts supporting a covering or roof, again much like that shown in the Mandeville illumination (colour plate 11). The presence of numerous fragments close by suggested that this was tile covered. The two sides of the main furnace were surrounded by a shallow gully, presumably to stop ground water running into the furnace itself. Also found in association with the furnace were the fragmentary remains of its roof. This appeared to have been constructed with a former of twigs covered in thick mud. On first firing the mud hardened and the twigs were burnt away, leaving a domed superstructure.

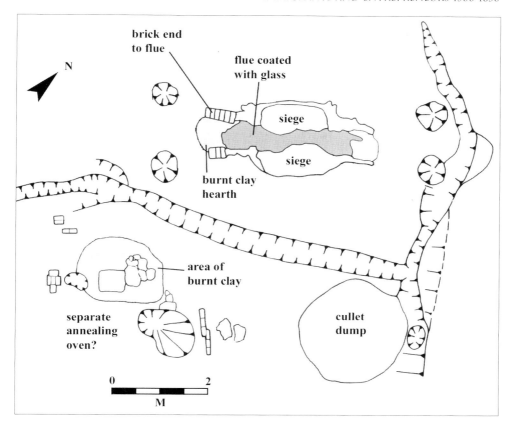

42 General plan of features at Bagot's Park. *After Crossley*

The remains of another oven were also found to the south and were separated by the gully. This was more ephemeral and disturbed than the other furnace, but was characterised by an oval patch of burning overlain, where they survived, with burnt flat-stone slabs. Also associated with this feature were some disturbed lines of brick and two postholes, although it is not possible to reconstruct this furnace further. Crossley suggested that this was probably an annealing oven, and there is no reason not to support this interpretation.

Other features were also associated with the complex. To the south-east of the main melting furnace was a large dump of cullet, as well as a much smaller one to the north-west. Also present to the north-east of furnace 1, on the other side of the gully (not shown on *42*) was a rectangular post-built building at least 4m long and just over 2m wide. Although clearly connected with the glassworks its exact function cannot be identified.

Also of interest were a large number of small stake holes arranged in a series of circular shapes 10m to 15m north-west of the main furnace. Thus far unique to any excavation of a glassmaking site, Crossley interpreted these as being racks for holding large window-glass crowns, and this interpretation is confirmed by analysis of the finds. The majority of the glass found consisted of edges and bull's-eyes from crown-glass sheets, and it seems probable that these were the main product. However, fragments from a number of vessels including beakers, flasks and handled tankards were also found. At the time of excavation it was thought that these were probably not products, but imported cullet. However, some of the glass initially classed as vessel glass can now be identified as blowing waste from vessel manufacture, suggesting that these may well have been products and not cullet.

Other finds from the site were typical of what might be expected. There were a large number of crucible fragments that were both barrel and bucket-shaped, following earlier medieval precursors. Also, unusually, fragments from two glassmaking tools were found. The first was a section of blowing iron, with some glass adhering internally, around 2cm in diameter and made from a rolled and welded wrought-iron sheet. The second was a thinner square-sectioned solid rod, probably a pontil iron.

The dating of Bagot's Park is crucial to the discussion of the decline of the glass industry in the first half of the sixteenth century and fortunately, due to good excavation techniques, this is possible. From samples of burnt clay from the base of the main furnace an archaeomagnetic date of 1535 $\pm$ 35yrs was calculated. This is confirmed by the associated ceramics from the site, which all belonged to the first half of the sixteenth century. Two interesting points arose from both excavations. Firstly, despite a sixteenth-century date, the crucibles being used at Bagot's Park, and to a certain extent Knightons, were essentially medieval in character, suggesting that they are a sensitive tool for differentiating earlier sixteenth-century 'transitional' sites from later ones. Secondly, the evidence for crown-glass production at both Bagot's and Knightons on a large scale suggests that Godfrey's assertion that window-glass production had ceased at this time was incorrect.

NEW ARRIVALS AND THE STIMULATION OF THE INDUSTRY

With the stagnation of the native English industry at a time when there was potentially a greater demand for glass than ever before, it is hardly surprising that there were those who saw an opportunity to fill a potentially profitable gap in the market. As there was an apparent inability by the English to seize this opportunity, it was only natural that the impetus for a revival in the glass industry was to come from abroad and be undertaken by the arrival of Northern European immigrants. The revival of the English industry by Protestant Flemish and Huguenot refugees is often commented upon, in particular by Eleanor Godfrey's *The Development of English Glassmaking 1560-1640*, which traces this in minute detail. However, it is sometimes forgotten that the influx of skilled refugees during the sixteenth century was not a phenomenon restricted to those knowledgeable in glassmaking. This was a time when a number of trades, such as the textile industry, were being affected by similar immigrant influences.

The impetus for the immigration of Protestant glassmakers was clearly related to religious and social persecution. Most notable was the St Bartholomew's Day Massacre, which began in Paris on 24 August 1572 and where over the following months up to 50,000 Protestant Huguenots are estimated to have been killed. However, even prior to this there were documented cases of immigrant glassmakers attempting to establish an industry. In 1549 eight Muranese were recorded as having arrived in London with the intention of setting up a furnace, but within two years all but one had returned, presumably in response to the threat of reprisals against their families by the Venetian authorities. The extent and success of their operation during this limited period is unknown. A few years later, in 1552, the merchant Henry

Smyth succeeded in securing a patent for twenty-one years to make 'brodeglass' using workers from Normandy, but there are no further records of this venture and it is unlikely that this was successful.

Jean Carré and Early Immigrant Glassworkers

The first successful attempt at reintroducing glassmaking in England is generally acknowledged to have been by Jean Carré. He originally came from Arras but was recorded to have resided in Antwerp for some years. There is still some debate whether he was actually a glassmaker himself, but it is clear that he knew glassmakers and was probably trained to some degree in the industry while in Antwerp. What was certain was that, in the spring of 1567, he arrived in London with sufficient capital and contacts to establish a glass furnace. Carré's decision to move from Antwerp was probably due to his Calvinist background and the fact his daughter was already living in London.

By July 1567 he had already secured a licence from the Crown to build two furnaces in the Weald at Fernfold, Alford and a further licence from the mayor and aldermen of the City of London to build one there. Carré was clearly very serious and organised about this venture, as even at this early date it was recorded that he had already ordered the soda for use in his furnaces. By 1567, presumably with his furnaces built and operational, Carré initially formed a company with Jean Chevalier, Peter Briet and Peter Appel, and soon after another Low Country merchant, Anthony Becku, joined the group. This company then petitioned the Crown for a monopoly to produce window glass, which was duly granted for twenty-one years on 8 September 1567, although a similar request for a monopoly controlling the production of Venetian-style crystal was refused. Importantly, the monopoly that Carré was granted contained the conditions that enough glass should be produced to satisfy the market, at a reasonable price and that, as part of the operation, there should be an effort made to teach the English the art of glassmaking.

With the monopoly in hand, Carré signed a contract in April 1568 with two Lorrainers, Thomas and Balthazar de Hennezell, to manage and co-own (along with four of their countrymen) one of the furnaces at Fernfold in the Weald. At the same time two Normandy glassmakers, Pierre and Jean de Bongard (known as Bungar in the contemporary documentation), were also contracted to run, but not co-own, the second furnace at Fernfold, specifically to make crown-window glass. Carré himself stayed in London, living at Broad Street, and seems to have concentrated his efforts on his crystal-glass furnace, which was built within the precinct of the old monastery of Crutched Friars, close to the Tower of London and manned by at least two Flemish glassmakers, John Levinion and Peter Cant.

However, even at this early date there were problems within Carré's company, caused by the issue of monopoly rights. The Flemish merchant Anthony Becku tried to assert his individual share of the monopoly rights. He appears to have been so unreasonable in some of his demands that he succeeded in making the Hennezells abandon their Fernfold furnace and return home. He also quarrelled with the Bungars, but they responded violently, driving away Becku's son, who had gone to visit them and injuring his agent James Arnold. Despite the Bungars being subsequently fined for this act, Becku seems to have lost interest in the running of the company and production appears to have continued to have been managed by Carré in London and the Bungars in the Weald.

Eleanor Godfrey has suggested that the London business may not have been initially very successful, for between 1570-71 Carré is recorded as bringing over the Venetians Quiobyn Littery and Giacomo (Jacob) Verzelini to help operate the furnace. This expansion in staffing continued and, by June 1571, six further Italians are recorded as living with, and presumably working for, Carré. Carré was clearly happy with the state of the London furnace at this stage, as he was confident enough to lease it to the Italians and went to Fernfold to build a new furnace for the production of drinking glasses in forest glass. However, before this project could get off the ground, Carré died in May 1572. His will charges that the project be continued, but it is uncertain whether this happened and it is probable that the last furnace was never built.

The company founded by Carré continued to operate after his death under the leadership of Briet and Appel, who took control of the window-glass monopoly. Despite this, the company appears to have been beset by problems. There was growing local resentment at the presence of foreign glassmakers in the Weald, while the company was beginning to suffer financially from the sales of imported glass. In an attempt to reverse their fortunes, Briet and Appel tried to negotiate for a new monopoly to ban the import of foreign glass. This was never granted; the company soon failed and the existing patent lapsed through non-observation. Interestingly, however, this was not disastrous to all those involved. The Bungars and their descendants continued to make window glass in the Weald until 1618, while production in London was soon to receive a new lease of life.

The Italian Influence

With the death of Jean Carré in May 1572, Jacob Verzelini took over the running of the Crutched Friars glasshouse. Despite being Italian by birth, Verzelini had worked for twenty-one years in the industry at Antwerp, where he had presumably first met Carré. While there he had married Elizabeth van Buren, the daughter of a minor Flemish noble (43). It is not certain whether Verzelini bought out Carré's London interests on his death, but he seems to have continued running the Crutched Friars furnace while the remaining members of the original company concentrated, ultimately unsuccessfully, on the Wealden window-glass monopoly.

Over the next two years Verzelini petitioned the Crown for, and eventually on 15 December 1574 received, a monopoly that gave him sole rights to manufacture drinking glasses in the Venetian style for twenty-one years. It was stipulated that he must sell his glasses 'as cheape or rather better cheape' than those that had previously been for sale, while the importation of similar wares was prohibited.

Business appears to have continued successfully for another year until 4 September 1575, when a fire broke out and completely destroyed the Crutched Friars furnace. Verzelini seems not to have been set back for long by this disaster; in 1576 he applied for, and was granted, naturalisation. With this new status, and the property rights that it brought, he was able to replace the furnace and build a new house, all within the confines of Crutched Friars.

It is interesting to note that more recent research, since Eleanor Godfrey's comprehensive study, has suggested that Verzelini might have intended to move part of his operations elsewhere shortly after the fire and the rebuilding at Crutched Friars. Civic records now held by the Corporation of London contain three references in October 1579 to a glasshouse that had been newly erected at Newgate Gaol. Of these, only one dated Tuesday 20 October specifically mentions Verzelini:

HERE LYETH BVRIED IACOB VERZELINI ESQVIRE BORNE IN THE CITTIE OF
VENICE, AND ELIZABETH HIS WIFE BORNE IN ANDWERPE OF THE AVN-
CIENT HOVSES OF VANBVREN AND MACE, WHO HAVINGE LIVED TOGE-
THER IN HOLYE STATE OF MATRIMONIE FORTIE NYNE YEARES AND
FOWER MONETHS. DEPARTED THIS MORTALL LYFE. THE SAID IACOB
THE TWENTYE DAY OF IANVARYE AN° DNI 1606. AGED LXXXIIII
YEARES. AND THE SAYD ELIZABETH THE XXVI DAYE OF OCTOBER
AN° DÑI 1607. AGED LXXIII YEARES
AND REST IN HOPE OF RESVRREXION TO LYFE ETERNALL.

43 Memorial brass in Downe church to Jacob and Elizabeth Verzelini.

> Item it ys orderyd that Mr. Sheryffes of this Cyttye shall presentlye cawse the glasshowse at Newgate latelye erected to be pulled downe. And ordered that Jacob Verselyne be heare the next Courte daye to gyve his direct aunsweare to this Courte wheather he wilbe content to enter into bond to the Chamberleyn of this Cyttye not to use his fornace duringe the tyme of this wunter for sparinge of wood and fewell.

On initial reading it appears that these two events must be related, and therefore it has been assumed that the Newgate Gaol furnace must have been erected by Verzelini. However, this need not be the case. After all, Verzelini was not being summoned to court on account of erecting the Newgate furnace; rather to make sure he was not operating his furnace during winter when fuel might be scarce, a common concern for this period. Indeed a further extract from thirteen days later on 2 November orders three aldermen to 'viewe this present afternoone the glassehouse lately erected by Jacob Verselyn estraunger (at) Crooched Fryers'. Here there is no mention of the Newgate furnace in connection with Verzelini, and it seems possible that another entrepreneur had built it. Indeed the very fact that its destruction was being ordered by the city authorities suggests that it was operating in contravention of Verzelini's monopoly.

If the Newgate furnace was a rival to Verzelini, it certainly was not the only one. In the late 1570s a glasshouse was built at Beckley near Rye by a Frenchman, Delaby, and an Italian, Orlandini. As it was established to make beads and bangles, it was not in contravention of Verzelini's monopoly. However, shortly after it was built it is clear that Orlandini broke the agreement, started producing vessel glass, and soon sold the business to John Smith, a glazier who moved operations to Ratcliffe in 1580. Verzelini legitimately complained about this breach of his monopoly and, in due course, the furnace was pulled down. This was probably a far from rare occurrence; for instance, it is known that, in 1586, Luthery, an Italian worker who trained at Crutched Friars, established his own furnace at Godalming, which also was subsequently suppressed. Other similar businesses probably operated without receiving much recorded attention, and seem to have had little effect on Verzelini's monopoly, which survived largely unchallenged until 1592.

Archaeological Evidence for Carré and Verzelini

It is unfortunate that, given the wealth of documentary evidence for glassmaking in the later sixteenth century, the archaeological sources are less forthcoming. Part of the reason for this is the location of some of the works in London. The Crutched Friars site has been continuously rebuilt and developed since the sixteenth century, and even on the unlikely chance that there are still any surviving remains of the furnace, these have yet to be found. A small quantity of glassmaking debris was found in the late nineteenth century at Smithfield, close to the site of the Carré and Verzelini furnaces, but it is far from certain that it originated there.

What Carré and Verzelini produced at Crutched Friars is also far from certain. Unlike the following century, there are no vessels found archaeologically that are distinctive enough to be suggested to be of English origin, although it is assumed that, because of his monopoly, Verzelini would have been producing high-quality drinking vessels such as goblets and beakers. Traditional art-historical scholarship has tried to link a number of complete vessels surviving in museum collections to Verzelini, often through the rather liberal interpretation of the historical evidence. The most commonly cited of these occurred in 1582 when a Frenchman, Anthony de Lysle, was naturalised and later, in 1583, when he was mentioned in the parish records of St Martin le Grand as being a 'graver in puter (pewter) and glasse'. This information has been linked with around a dozen or so glasses that do survive intact and are indeed decorated with engraved designs and bearing dates in the 1580s. However, engraving was a decorative technique used in a number of glassmaking centres and, more importantly, there is no record that de Lysle actually worked for Verzelini, and he may have just been an engraver of window glass. Of the intact glasses normally attributed to Verzelini, some are almost certainly of foreign manufacture, although others are more typical of those found archaeologically, indeed some are even engraved in English rather than Latin (*front cover*). Whatever the case may be, even if these glasses are presumed to have been manufactured at Crutched Friars, they can only provide a limited representation of Verzelini's total repertoire.

A little more is known about Carré's two furnaces at Fernfold in the Weald. Examination of the records relating to the manor of Bury records that Fernfold Wood was rented 'to divers strangers being glassmakers' for the sum of £35 and that they had 'two houses to make glasse in'. Winbolt located the site of one of these furnaces in 1935, but it was heavily truncated and he only made a sketch plan of it (*44*). He recorded its overall measurements as being 10ft x 20ft with a central sandstone-lined flue just over 2ft wide and with two brick-built sieges. At either end were two brick-floored hearths bounded at either end by 'stokers' platforms of brick. Winbolt only found a couple of fragments of glass and it was not possible to characterise the output of the furnace.

On the rather slight evidence that was recorded, this furnace appears to be similar to earlier Wealden designs, although the use of brick in the sieges was an innovation. However, some caution must be exercised due to the sketchiness of his plan. Interestingly,

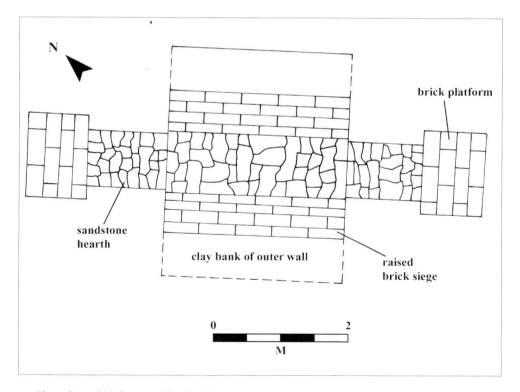

44 Plan of Fernfold furnace. *After Winbolt*

Kenyon suggested that the location of the second documented furnace might lie only 400m away. He points to the find of a large concentration of glass fragments in Sandpit Field at Barnford, the name of which he suggests is a corruption of Fernfold, in 1961. However he acknowledged that there was no other signs of furnace structure or even burning here, and the glass was largely undiagnostic blowing waste.

Other Immigrants in the Weald

With the effective failure of the Wealden window-glass monopoly after Carré's death in 1572, there would have been few impediments to other immigrant glassmakers wanting to establish operations in the Weald. While it is known that the Bungars continued to operate at Fernfold into the seventeenth century, other families can also be identified. Kenyon, in his comprehensive trawl of the parish records for the area, identified a number of possible glassmaking families. These included the Cacquerays and Titterys from the 1570s onwards, who were increasingly mentioned, particularly centring on the parish of Wisborough. Other parishes had names, such as the Tysacks at Ewhurst, that were to subsequently play significant roles in the English glass industry. Interestingly, there were no immigrants that could be associated with glassmaking in the records of Chiddingfold parish, which had previously been the centre of English manufacture, and it appears that the Peytowe family were still operating there. However, in all these cases it has not been possible to definitively link any of these families and a known archaeological site.

Despite this, both Winbolt and Kenyon identified a number of Wealden sites that they described as 'late' or belonging to the later sixteenth or early seventeenth centuries (45). These later sites, primarily characterised by a better quality of glass found at them, were clustered mainly in Wisborough Green and Loxwood parishes. Most have only been identified by scatters of glassmaking waste and crucibles, although two were investigated by Winbolt that had structural remains.

No.	Name	Parish	Condition 1991-93
4	Lower Chaleshurst	Chiddingfold	Destroyed
8	Imbhams	Chiddingfold	Unknown
9	Pickhurst	Chiddingfold	Unknown
14	Glasshouse Lane	Kirdford	Surviving
22	Barnfold Farm	Loxwood	Unknown
23	Brookland	Wisborough Green	Surviving
24	Burchetts	Loxwood	Surviving
25	Fernfold	Loxwood	Surviving
26	Horsebridge	Wisborough Green	Surviving
27	Gunshot	Loxwood	Surviving
30	Sponghurst	Loxwood	Unknown
32	Woodhouse Farm	Loxwood	Surviving
35	Vann Copse	Hambledon	Surviving
36	Ellen's Green	Ewhurst	Destroyed

37	Somersbury	Ewhurst	Surviving
38	Sidney Wood	Alfold	Surviving
40	Petworth Park	Lurgashall	Surviving

45 Table of 'late' glassmaking sites in the Weald. *Adapted from Kenyon*

The first of these, at Sidney Wood, Alford, was very close to the earlier site of Knightons. Winbolt dug there in 1930-31, but unfortunately he only recorded the barest details of what he found, and no plan survives. He notes a rectangular structure 30ft-40ft long and 20ft wide, although this would seem very large compared with an ordinary furnace. He made few other structural observations, save that the sieges were made from brick, so the overall form of the furnace is a mystery. He also recovered a large quantity of glass, which Kenyon subsequently remarked was the finest quality he had seen from any Wealden site. This primarily consisted of vessel glass, with forms including pedestal-footed beakers and goblets, although there were also some pieces from windows. Fragments of Germanic stoneware found in association with the structure suggest that it was in use during the last decades of the sixteenth century.

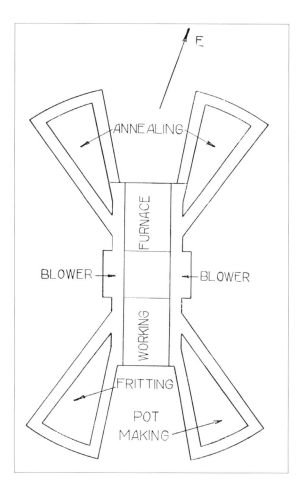

46 Plan of the Vann furnace. *S. Winbolt*

seige

wing

seige

flue

wing

47 The Vann furnace under excavation. Note the spade is standing in one of the projecting 'wings'. *Winbolt*

The other furnace dating to this later period was investigated by Winbolt in 1931 at Vann Copse. This was rather better preserved and his sketch plan and photographs enable a more accurate reconstruction (*46, 47*). It is clearly a rectangular brick-built furnace with two distinct sieges or 'shelves', as Winbolt described them, and a projecting flue. Also apparent from his records are four diagonally orientated wings with internal chambers, which Winbolt probably correctly suggested were for the annealing and possible fritting processes. Although there is no scale on his plan, one interesting aspect of this furnace is the small size of the main working area; it would seem there was only space on each siege for one or maybe two crucibles. This might in part be explained by Winbolt's rather stylistic recording of the furnace, but the photograph does seem to indicate that this was the case. Unfortunately, little glass was recovered during the excavation to help date the furnace, but from its form it must date to the late sixteenth century. Interestingly, in the 1950s, some references to glassmaking on the Burgate estate, within which bounds the Vann furnace used to be situated, were found. These referred on 8 December 1586 to Ognybene Luthery, a Venetian who had 'of late erected a house, furnace, and oven in the wood of Henry Smyth gent. of Burgate'. That Ognybene Luthery is the same man as Quiobyn Littery, who was brought over by Carré in 1571 as part of the team to work his Crutched Friars furnace, can be of little doubt. However, whether the Vann furnace, or another as yet undiscovered glasshouse, can be directly related to him is less certain. Nonetheless the two were contemporaneous, so it remains an interesting possibility.

Immigrants Outside of the Weald

While the Weald, with its pre-existing tradition of glassmaking, was an obvious location for early immigrant activities, the industry was not restricted to this area for long. Certainly glassmaking was taking place in a number of locations in the South-East of England, often in connection with specific building projects. In 1570 John Lennard obtained the lease of the Knole Estate in Kent. Soon after, it was documented that he had established a furnace for a period of two to three years specifically to supply window glass for the Mansion House. Although there are no archaeological remains that can be identified, a number of household accounts survive. These note that, between 27 July 1585 and 18 January 1585/86, 425 carts of wood for the purpose of glassmaking, costing a total of 75*l* 6*s* 8*d*, were brought to the estate. Just the next month on 19 February, materials for the construction of the furnace are described, and these included:

ij lode pot clay for making xij pots
j lode of bryk clay for making bryks
iiij stones for making an oven
iij syles
ij payles
ij shovels
j colvet
a whele barrow
iiij bushels of fretyng glas
and vj pypes as apereth by hys bylle

While some of these elements are hard to quantify, this list of building materials and equipment is of particular interest and it demonstrated that the construction of the structures was carefully planned. Perhaps most intriguing was the reference to four bushels of 'fretyng' glass. This might refer to cullet collected to be remelted, or it could suggest that pre-made frit was brought to the site to be melted into a final fully fused glass. Subsequent estate records suggest a number of glassmakers successfully produced window glass there in 1587, and the listed names of Oneby, Valyan and Bousell suggest that these were of immigrant origin.

Another site where there is both documentary and archaeological evidence for immigrant activity is at Buckholt, Hampshire, located around ten miles to the east of Salisbury. There are several interesting references in the register of the Walloon church in Southampton that link glassmaking with this village. On 7 October 1576 Jan du Tisac, Pierre Vaillant and Claude Potier were described as '*ouvriers de verre a la verriere de Boucehaut*' ('glassworkers from the glasshouse at Buckholt'). There were several similar references, the last of which dates to 4 January 1579/80, when Monsieur du Hou '*verrieren a Bouquehaut*' was admitted to communion. These all clearly suggest that, during the 1570s, glassmaking was taking place in the parish, and Kenyon identifies two possible sites in the vicinity of Buckholt that are probably related to these men.

One of these was discovered and cleared by the Reverend E. Kell in 1860. His records are relatively scant, but he did draw a plan (*48*). He noted an oblong brick furnace 4ft 9in x 6ft externally. This was surrounded by a number of irregular detached stone walls, the function of which Kell clearly did not understand. The whole site was encompassed by a shallow ditch. With hindsight it is now possible to reconstruct this furnace as one very similar to Vann, having a central melting furnace and four attached 'wings' for subsidiary glassmaking activities. This style of the winged furnace appears to be a clear

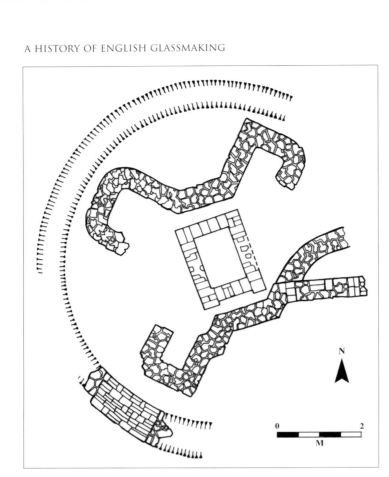

48 Plan of the furnace at Buckholt. *After Kell*

indication of Huguenot construction, and one that typifies later sixteenth and early seventeenth-century furnaces. Kell also found a large quantity of window glass during his excavation, and this was the likely output of the furnace, although vessels might also have been made.

Another Hampshire site close to the Weald, about ten miles to the west of Lurgashall, is at Buriton. The Revered P. Gallup, who recognised the significance of the name Glasshouse Paddock on the 1841 tithe map, first identified the site. Fragments of glass and low mounds indicated the location of the site and, between 1971-72, staff of Portsmouth City Museum undertook excavations on an area 20m square. Dated by clay pipes to the last quarter of the sixteenth century, there was certainly clear evidence for glassworking such as crucibles, working waste and stones covered with glass. However, the excavated structure on first sight appears rather confusing and unlike any other furnace thus far excavated (49).

The explanation of its odd appearance lies in the fact that there were at least two phases of use on the site. The first appears to have taken the form of a simple rectangular furnace with a central flue 75cm-80cm wide. Although subsequently heavily disturbed, from the extent of surface burning the overall furnace was only around 2m-2.5m long, although no siege benches survived. The second phase saw the demolition of the furnace, and the original flue was lined with stone and vaulted with reused brick splashed with glass. The whole structure was then covered with a mortar spread, into which was set a stone platform, edged on the eastern end by brick. The function of the second phase is

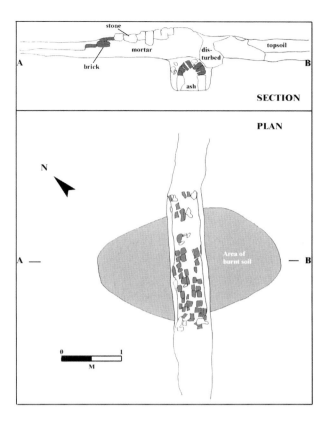

49 Plan of the furnace at
Buriton. *After Fox and Lewis*

unclear, and may well not relate to glassmaking, but it appears that the original flue had
now been turned into a drain.

Later, in 1976, a second furnace was discovered 500m to the north-east by John
Cooper, but unfortunately this went virtually unrecorded. It too appears to have been
heavily disturbed and only represented by a flue, although little more is known of it.
Finds from both sites included crucibles and glass that seemed to suggest that cylinder
window glass was made here, although the fragment of a tankard handle in a similar
metal also might suggest vessel production as well.

There is no direct documentary evidence for who may have been working this
furnace. But there is an interesting coincidence. Between 1567-79 a William Overton
was the rector of the parish here. In itself this means little, except that, later on in his
career, Overton became the Bishop of Coventry & Lichfield, when it is known he was
directly responsible for the establishment of a glasshouse at Bishop's Wood, Eccleshall
(discussed below). While there is nothing but his proximity to link him with the Buriton
furnace, it is tempting to suggest that this was an earlier venture of his.

Early Immigrant Glassmaking in Staffordshire and Lancashire

Earlier sixteenth-century evidence for glassmaking at Wolseley and Bagot's Park in
Staffordshire has already been discussed. However, it is clear that this tradition continued
into the later sixteenth century and more extensive manuscript sources survive for this

period. One dated 5 June 1585 records the agreement between Richard Bagot and Ambrose Hensey, whereby a glasshouse was to be erected by Bagot, the cost of which would be paid back by Hensey within a year either in cash or in the equivalent value of glass. Bagot also undertook to supply sufficient wood from his estate for the venture. Another document, written twenty-one days later on 26 June, records the testimonial of Thomas Plyter, bailiff of Eccleshall Castle and employee of the Bishop of Coventry & Lichfield. In this, he grants Edward Hensey the glassmaker permission 'to leave the lordship's glasshouse' after Hensey had been involved in a dispute with his brother. Ambrose and Thomas Hensey almost certainly must be members of the Hennezell family, first brought to England by Carré, and it is possible to suggest how they came to be in Staffordshire in the 1580s.

Plyter describes the glasshouse as belonging to his lordship, which at this time was the same William Overton who had earlier been rector at Buriton. Furthermore, while still rector at Buriton, Overton was also recorded as a canon at Salisbury Cathedral in 1573. Given his documented career, Pape, and in more recent years Russell Fox and Elizabeth Lewis, have linked the spread of some immigrant glassmakers to the enterprises of Overton. They suggested that, on Carré's death in 1572, Overton encouraged some of the immigrant glassmakers to establish furnaces, not only at Buriton where he was rector, but maybe also at Buckholt, which was, after all, only a few miles from where he was as a canon at Salisbury. Pape then suggested that, on his promotion to Bishop of Coventry & Lichfield, Overton encouraged at least some glassmakers to establish a furnace near his residence of Eccleshall Castle. If this credible explanation is indeed the case, then it acts as an interesting illustration of how one man's direct patronage was instrumental in encouraging the spread of glassmaking into a variety of new areas.

While the documentary sources indicate there was glassmaking in the later sixteenth century in this area of Staffordshire, there is also archaeological evidence as well. T. Pape undertook quite a considerable amount of work in the 1920s and 1930s trying to identify glassmaking sites in the wooded area of north Staffordshire between Market Drayton and Eccleshall. Through extensive fieldwork, he identified a number of possible working sites that appeared to date to the later sixteenth and early seventeenth centuries. Some consisted of just ephemeral finds of crucible fragments, such as at Broughton Hall; in other cases he also looked at the place-name evidence, in 1929 investigating 'Glass House Farm' near Knowle Wood, where he found reused blocks of sandstone, originally part of a furnace, built into barn walls as well as glass in the farm precinct. The following year, less than a mile away at Glasshouse Croft, Pape recorded probing and finding a furnace base, but unfortunately he did not describe it in any further.

However, Pape's most interesting investigations were at the north end of Bishop's Wood (also known as Blore Park). From the Eccleshall parish records he noted that, between 1600-04, four different glassmakers were connected with the immediate area, such as a John Esquire, glassmaker of 'Blower Parke'. Prompted by this, in 1931 Pape investigated three mounds on the edge of the woods. One of these was heavily disturbed by a tree, although the other two survived better. In one, Pape found a largely intact furnace that was built-up off the ground with large square blocks of sandstone. In the centre was a flue 20in wide with an intact arched opening on its western end (50). Inside the furnace were two siege benches 2ft 10in long, 1ft high and 16in wide, and fused to one of these were the remains of bases from two large melting crucibles, and a smaller 'test pot' on the other. But most interesting is that much of the superstructure had survived up to a height of 3ft above the ground, and consisted of vertical sandstone walls rising to just below the now-missing vaulted ceiling. Unfortunately, Pape made less reference to any

50 The furnace at Bishop's Wood under excavation. *Pape*

finds that he encountered. He does mention window glass, and also alludes to drinking vessels and bottles, and the glass was apparently of a very high quality, again confirming a late sixteenth or early seventeenth-century date. While it is impossible to tell whether this furnace excavated by Pape is the same as the one recorded as being worked by either the Henseys or any other immigrants, it does provide confirmatory evidence for renewed glassmaking during this period in Staffordshire.

Another Staffordshire site that can be dated to this period of immigrant glassmaking is that of Little Birches at Wolseley. The evidence for medieval glassmaking here and at nearby Cattail Pool has already been outlined in chapter three, but while undertaking these excavations in 1991-92 Christopher Walsh also revealed the remains of a later sixteenth-century glassworks. These features lay 30-40m south of the earlier fourteenth-century furnace and took the form of low mounds. The largest of these on excavation proved to be a large, well-preserved structure, furnace 1 (*51*). Constructed of sandstone, it was 4.3m long and 2.2m wide with a central flue 55cm in breadth. The two sieges were intact, measuring 1.6m x 0.4m, and each had the remains of three fused crucible bases still remaining on them (*colour plate 16*). Interestingly, the ends of each flue were constructed from brick and just beyond each of these was dug a shallow scoop, each with a pair of substantial postholes cut through. The precise function of these pits and postholes remains uncertain, but it is possible that they related to some form of furnace covering.

Furnace 2, by contrast, was more ephemeral and different in form. Although more disturbed, it was roughly 1.6m square and constructed from sandstone blocks that, on two sides, had been completely rubbed away. It was filled internally with a charcoal spread and broken glass and was interpreted as an annealing oven. After the main

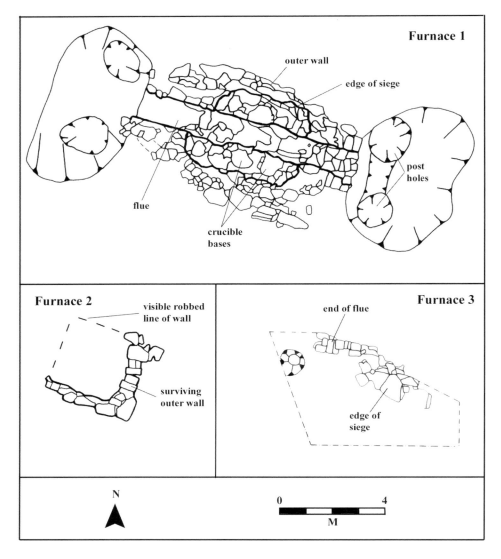

51 Furnaces 1–3 at Little Birches, Wolseley. *After Welsh*

excavation and during subsequent groundworks, remains of a third structure, furnace 3, was disturbed. Although only partially investigated, enough was revealed to suggest it took the same form as furnace 1 (*51*). A siege edge, the end of the flue and a large external posthole were all recorded.

Surrounding the glass furnaces, large ash, waste and glass tips could clearly be identified and were sampled. Fragments of crucibles were numerous, and interestingly these had a distinctive out-turned rather than a vertical rim. A large quantity of glass was also recovered, although only sixty-six fragments came from vessels, primarily earlier flasks and urinals, suggesting this was collected cullet. What were more numerous were fragments of window glass, which, from the large number of curved edge pieces, indicated they had been made by the crown method.

The later sixteenth-century glassmaking at Little Birches is important as it helps provide further detail to the emerging picture for the region. However, it does raise nearly as many questions as it answers. Unfortunately, and contrasting with the nearby sites at Bagot's Park, there is no documentation that can be connected with this site at this particular time. Therefore, it cannot be definitively said that this site was built and run by immigrant glassmakers, although in all likelihood it was. A further complicating matter was the rather unusual design of furnaces 1 and 3. On one hand, neither had evidence for attached wings as might be expected, based on other immigrant-style furnaces at Vann or Buckholt, but on the other their design is markedly different from any earlier English types in the region or nationally.

Also worthy of brief mention is another glassmaking site dating to the very end of the century in the North-West, this time at Bickerstaffe near Ormskirk in Lancashire. Although both the historical and archaeological sources are largely absent, this site is important as it shows immigrant glassmakers had reached this area by at least 1600, and established the foundations of what was to become a more significant regional industry in subsequent centuries. The only historical reference to glassmaking at Bickerstaffe can be found in the parish register for Ormskirk when on 10 December 1600 was recorded the burial of 'a stranger slayne by one of the glassemen beinge a ffrenchman working at Bycerstaff'.

The location of this furnace was identified by the name Glass Hey field on the tithe map, and field walking in 1968 revealed a scatter of crucible fragments and glass there. Excavations in this area revealed the foundations of a heavily disturbed furnace base, possibly deliberately dismantled, and further truncated by subsequent ploughing. Its form was largely unclear, being generally indicated by a patch of burning. However, the stone-lined flue was still intact and this was angled in a westerly direction to catch the prevailing wind. Running away from the furnace was a clear line of demolition debris that included a significant quantity of crucible and glass waste. It was clear from this waste that vessel glass was the main product, and a range of forms such as pedestal beakers and goblets, small flasks and jugs were produced, as well as sleek stones and decorative flower prunts, glass typical of immigrant manufacture (see below). The Bickerstaffe glasshouse appears to have been short-lived, perhaps the result of the documented murder, and glassmaking moved elsewhere in the county.

Immigrant Glassmaking in Hereford and Gloucestershire

While it is recognised that immigrant glassmakers moved to the North-West, possibly under the patronage of William Overton, it is also clear they rapidly spread to other areas of the country in the late sixteenth century. One of most interesting and yet still under-researched of these areas is the South-West of England, and Hereford and Gloucestershire in particular. Unfortunately, little documentation for the late sixteenth and early seventeenth centuries has been found for this area, although this might well be due to the lack of the same intensive investigation that the Weald and Staffordshire have received.

One site that is of particular interest and dates to this period is at St Weonards, halfway between Hereford and Monmouth. The general position of the site was indicated by the name Glasshouse Farm, but it was first more specifically located by Basil Marmont in 1922, who found fragments of glass and crucible on the ground. The area was later revisited by N. Bridgewater in 1959, who again found significant quantities of glass to the south of the farm. His initial trial trenching in this area proved unsuccessful in identifying the furnace, until in 1961 an early magnetometer survey located a specific spot of intense burning, and this was subject to excavation. What was revealed was a circular patch of burning, but without any evidence for sieges or any other superstructure (52). The only surviving feature was an east-west running metalled surface about a metre wide, and this was the remains of the base of the flue. Given these very ephemeral features, it was clear that the furnace had been destroyed and almost completely removed after it had ceased to function. To the south of the furnace there was evidence for a small semi-circular ditch cut into the upslope, presumably to prevent the flow of ground water into the furnace.

Also in association with the main furnace, and directly to the west of it, was a patch of burnt material and charcoal, presumably the raking-out of material from the flue. The only other interesting feature was a brick-built structure to the south-east of, but still adjoining, the main patch of burning. As with the other features, this had been all but destroyed and survived only in places and to a single course of bricks in height. At the time of excavation this feature was interpreted as a separate free-standing structure,

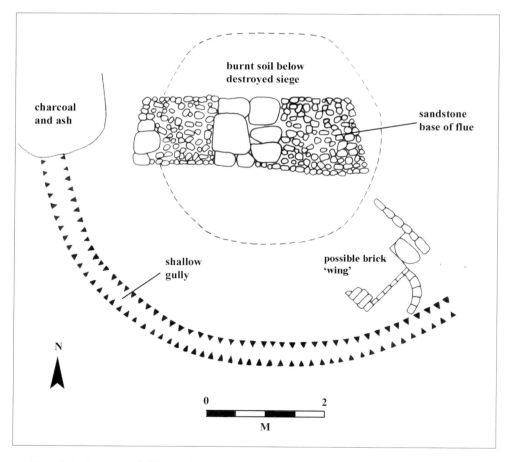

52 Plan of the furnace at St Weonards. *After Bridgewater*

possibly an annealing oven. However, its proximity and orientation to the main furnace is strange, and a better interpretation might be that it was the very ephemeral remains of an attached wing in the style of the Vann furnace, the traces of the other three having been completely removed by subsequent levelling. Whether this was definitely an immigrant-style furnace is not certain, but the glass found included pedestal and cylindrical beakers, crown-window glass and other waste, and was certainly consistent with their repertoire. It is therefore regrettable that, as yet, there are no documentary sources confirming the presence of Lorrainers in the location, but it seems likely that they were indeed working at St Weonards.

Another site that has better documentary evidence for glassmaking is at the hamlet of Glasshouse, Newent, midway between Ross-on-Wye and Gloucester. The parish records for Newent contained a number of references to glassmakers and their families, the first of which, on 2 February 1597/8 mentions the baptism of the daughter of 'Mr Bridgeman of the glasshouse'. Who this individual was is uncertain, but it might be that he was the English owner of the glasshouse rather than one of its workers. Certainly in the succeeding years there were further baptismal records that refer to members of a number of established immigrant glassmaking families. On 12 August 1599 'John Pylme a Frenchman of the glasshouse'; on 20 October 1599 'Tyzack Abram sonne of a Frenchman of the glasshouse' and on 24 February 1600/1 'Margaret, daughter of Anthony Voyden glass founder' were all baptised. The presence of members of the Pilmey, Tyzack and Voyden families suggests that quite a considerable operation was afoot here, and such a concentration of births in these years might indicate that the glasshouse was recently established and successful enough that the workers felt settled enough to start families. How long the furnace was in operation for is uncertain, but it seems to have been some time. As late as 1634 in his will, John Bulnoys of Newent bequeathed to his eldest son 'all my moulds and tools for making glass whatsoever'. The last reference in the parish records is to the marriage of John Gulney, 'glassmaker of Newent', in 1638, although it is likely that the furnace ceased operations shortly after this.

Archaeological evidence for the furnace is less forthcoming. No structural remains have been found, but the rough location in a field in Glasshouse hamlet was identified in 1968 when groundwork revealed the presence of crucibles, waste glass and vessels. Alan Vince summarised this material, which contains the expected range of pedestal and cylindrical beakers, but also interestingly vessels with flower prunts and handled sleek stones.

The third and final site identified in this region lies in Woodchester Park, near the village of Nailsworth just south of Stroud. This site is one of the best known and yet most unusual in the whole of England, as well as being the least understood. Frustratingly, no direct documentary evidence has been found that can be related to this site and shed light on which families were working there. Given the size and apparent sophistication of this furnace, this is unusual. One possibility is that there might be a connection with the de Houx family. It was noted in the letters patent obtained in 1592 by Sir Jerome Bowes that in Gloucestershire 'one Hoe a Frenchman, hath built a glass house and furnace and doth make great quantities of glasses'. However, there is no direct link between this reference and Woodchester, and the only evidence is circumstantial. As the de Houx family are not mentioned in the Newent parish records and Woodchester is the only other known glasshouse of this date in Gloucestershire, it seems possible that this reference might be tentatively linked with this site. There is only a single reference in the Nailsworth parish records that can be linked to the site, that being in 1613 to 'William Mason of the glasshouse'.

The site of the Woodchester furnace was discovered in 1877 by Basil Marmont who, as a fifteen-year-old boy, claimed he came across it while searching for his lost ferret. From then on he periodically visited the site and collected pieces of glass. In 1904 W. St Clair Baddeley, aided by the glass historian Albert Hartshorne, visited the site and undertook a survey and limited excavation, which was published in 1920. However, the site is more commonly associated with Stuart Daniels' 1950 book *The Woodchester Glasshouse*. Unfortunately this presents a confused and at times inaccurate description of the site, and it is particularly interesting that Daniels only acknowledges Baddeley's report once, which he describes as being 'in very general terms and says practically nothing about the products'. This is in fact curious, as the plan of the site published by Daniels, and clearly based on Baddeley's, is only partially complete and not half as informative. It is also regrettable that Kenyon seems to have been unaware of Baddeley's work and again only reproduces Daniels' plan.

The actual site lies in Collier's Wood just outside of the boundary of the later park created by Sir George Huntley between 1617-20. Despite being continuously wooded since at least the seventeenth century and probably long before, the site remains clearly visible today. It sits on a central spur bounded on either side by natural runnels. There is an artificially cut platform roughly 15m x 30m, on which the most visible feature is a large annular mound that remains virtually unaltered since it was first photographed in 1904 (53). On excavation this feature proved to be about 5m in diameter, with walls 1m thick. Baddeley did not record what they were constructed from, but his illustration suggests brick. This plan also suggests the presence of four evenly spaced openings, a little above ground level, although in the text he refers to just two of them (54).

53 The Woodchester glasshouse in 1904. *Baddeley*

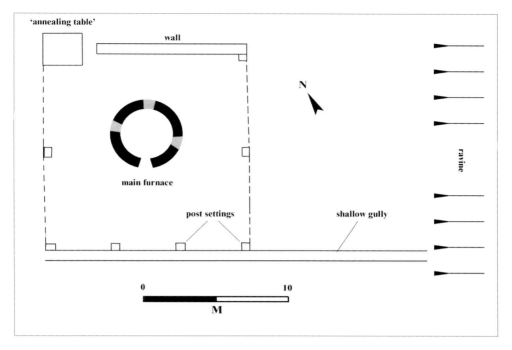

54 Plan of the Woodchester glasshouse. *After Baddeley*

From this plan and description, the furnace at Woodchester appears to be very different from any other known in England, apparently being circular and of Southern European type. However, the Woodchester example is very different from any excavated Italian furnaces, being significantly wider and with more substantial walls. Baddeley's excavation also indicated that there were the remains of a covering building. On the north side he identified a possible wall with an entrance, while on the other sides post-pads indicated the presence of a timber post-built structure that drained to a gully on the southern side. One further feature noted in 1904 was a rectangular structure in the north-west corner that measured 9ft x 7ft, which was described at the time as an 'annealing table', although it is far from certain that it served this function. A recent survey of the site has also indicated that there may be further structural features. On the southern side, just upslope of the terrace cut, is a collapsed wall and a possible house platform, maybe for a dwelling associated with the furnace. To both the east and west sides of the main furnace feature are two large tips of crucible, glass and waste.

The glass found by Marmont and Baddeley falls into two distinctive categories. The first is a typical green glass, and was used to make windows through the cylinder process, and this is usually quite heavily weathered. However, the majority of the vessel glass recovered was made in a much better quality blue/green metal that in some cases suffered no weathering at all. Vessels made in this metal include the usual range of pedestal beakers and goblets as well as distinctive rosette prunts similar to those found at Newent (*55*), although again the form of vessel they decorated is unclear. Further typological connections with Newent are evidenced by several pieces of handled linen smoothers noted by Baddeley.

55 Glass found by Baddeley at Woodchester. *Daniels*

Immigrant Glassmaking in North-East England

While a number of other parts of the country also have fragmentary evidence for early immigrant glassmaking, one area that is worthy of brief note is North Yorkshire. Two sites dating to the last quarter of the sixteenth century have been excavated by David Crossley at Hutton Common and Rosedale Valley, both of which lie in the parish of Lastingham. Unfortunately the documentary evidence for the region is again scarce, save for a single entry in the parish records on 2 March 1592/3. Here is mentioned 'uxor Amabie glassman' and this fleeting reference to the wife of a French glassmaker does not adequately reflect the archaeological evidence for this parish, which is, by contrast, quite spectacular.

The first of the two sites was identified at Hutton Common in the late 1960s when bracken clearance revealed glassmaking debris and furnace structures that were still standing relatively tall because the site had never been ploughed (*colour plate 17*). The most obvious of these features was a rectangular melting furnace, which had gone through three different phases of use and alteration (*56*). In its first phase the furnace was relatively simple, measuring around 3m square with a central stone-lined flue. The furnace was constructed from stone packed in boulder clay and had two hearths either end of the flue. A substantial rebuilding marked the second phase, which resulted in the attachment of two diagonally opposed wings to the south-west and north-east. During this phase the furnace was then surrounded by a small gully to prevent the flow of ground water. The final phase was marked by a complete reconstruction. The central block was rebuilt, this time partly using brick, which itself underwent subsequent repair. Also during this phase a much larger bank and ditch were cut on the western side of the furnace, and postholes to the north and south suggest there was a lightweight covering or roof. This last phase also saw the construction of a second smaller furnace 3m to the west, which was much more disturbed and of less certain form. This has been interpreted

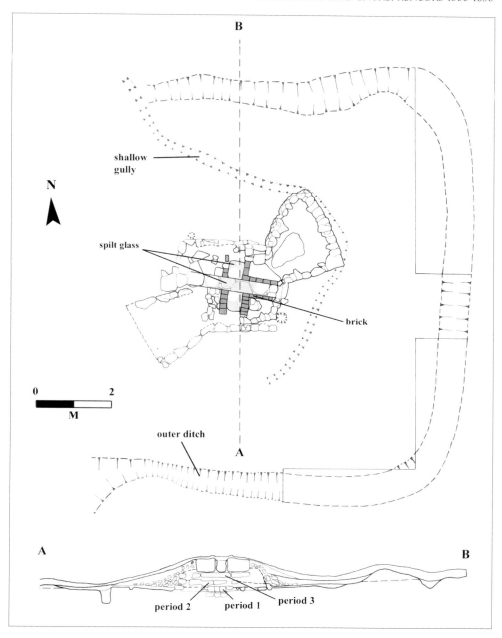

B

shallow
gully

N

spilt glass

brick

0   2
M

outer ditch

A

A

B

period 2   period 1   period 3

56 Plan of the Hutton furnace. *After Crossley*

as an annealing oven. Finally, to both the north and south, two large dumps of glass, waste and crucible were identified and sampled.

The other site in Rosedale Valley was discovered in 1966, and when the ground was cleared of scrub two mounds could clearly be seen (57). On excavation one of these was shown to be the main furnace which, although appeared to date to a single phase, was a large and complex structure (*colour plate 18*). It was similar in width to Hutton (around 3m) but it was longer with a north-south running flue, and sieges that were constructed from quite small stones set in a clay bond. Unlike Hutton it had four attached and splayed wings, although interestingly it appears that during the course of the furnace's operation the north-eastern one was demolished.

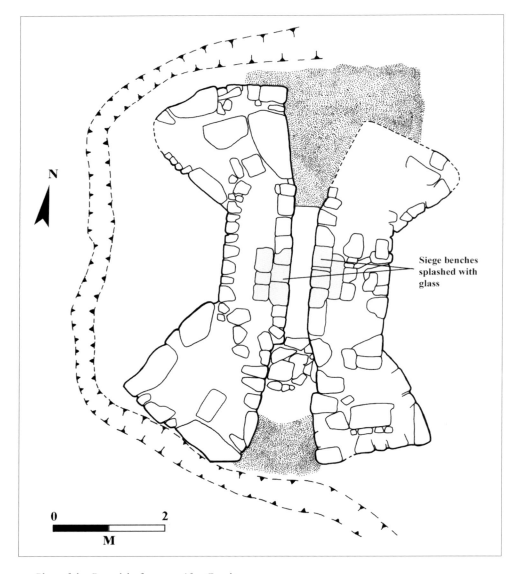

Siege benches splashed with glass

N

0 — 2
M

57 Plan of the Rosedale furnace. *After Crossley*

Also of interest at Rosedale were the features around the main furnace (58). These consisted of other stone-built structures both interpreted as annealing ovens. One, furnace A, was of clay construction, faced with stone and divided into two halves, although there was no surviving evidence of how the structure could have been heated. The other, furnace B, survived rather better and had a more obvious form. At ground level it had a stone-capped flue and the stone, which formed a platform, had clearly been exposed to prolonged burning. What, however, was less certain was the function of these subsidiary ovens at Rosedale, a question that might also be asked of Hutton. It is usually reasoned that, with the winged immigrant-style furnace, subsidiary activities such as fritting and annealing took place within the wing structures.

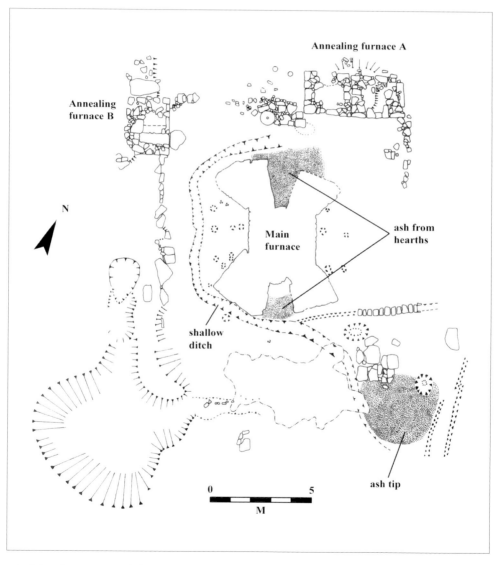

58 Other features around the Rosedale furnace. *After Crossley*

93

Other features around the Rosedale furnace are of interest. These included a shallow drain on the north, west and south sides of the main furnace, as well as post holes to the east and west, that altogether might suggest the presence of a pitched roof over the structure. Also of note was the identification of a contemporary small two-room cottage just a short distance from the working floor. If the two were linked, it is a clear indication that the glassmakers were living as well as working on site. At Rosedale and more particularly Hutton a significant quantity of finds were recovered. These included a large amount of crucibles and waste glass, which seemed to have come exclusively from vessel manufacture, as opposed to being collected cullet. The range of forms included pedestal and cylindrical beakers, pedestal goblets, small bottles and other diverse types, and again there were also rosette prunts and fragments of linen smoothers on both sites.

THE ENGLISH INTERVENTION IN THE INDUSTRY

Because Verzelini's patent to make Venetian-style drinking glasses did not cover either green vessel glass or window glass, the expansion of Huguenot production across England in the later sixteenth century had not constituted a breach of his monopoly rights. Indeed it appears that Verzelini had experienced few problems or direct competition, which allowed him to prosper and buy an estate at Knowle in Kent. However, perhaps it was inevitable that seeing a foreigner, albeit a naturalised one, successfully amassing a fortune would lead to others attempting to take over his monopoly rights. This finally happened in 1592 when, with the old patent still having three years to run, a prominent courtier Sir Jerome Bowes was awarded by the Crown a virtually identical revision of Verzelini's patent to produce Venetian-style glass for twelve years once Verzelini's had expired in December 1595. A further incentive for this reissuing of the patent was that Bowes, unlike Verzelini, now had to pay the Crown 66*l* 15*s* annually for this privilege. Perhaps under pressure, Verzelini retired prematurely in 1592, although his sons Francis and Jacob continue to work the Crutched Friars furnace.

William Robson, Jerome Bowes and Edward Zouch

On the expiry of Verzelini's patent Bowes set about building a furnace at the site of the old Black Friars monastery, which he rented off Sir George More for this purpose in March 1595/6. It would seem that Verzelini's sons would not accept the cessation of their own monopoly and unsuccessfully tried to challenge the legality of Bowes' patent. To help bolster his authority in this matter Bowes took on a London entrepreneur, William Robson, to manage his glass monopoly, and he was so successful in this regard that Bowes eventually succeed in getting both Francis and Jacob imprisoned and effectively removed from the glassmaking industry for good.

But shortly after Robson and Bowes had secured their rights against the Verzelinis there were to be other infringements. Despite Robson securing an extension to Bowe's original patent for a further twenty-one years in October 1605, just three years later a company headed by Edward Salter was granted a second monopoly to make 'all manner of drinking glasses, and other glasse and glasse workes not prohibited by former letters patent'. They constructed a furnace at Winchester House, Southwark and started producing vessels not included in Bowes' monopoly, including dishes and salts, but more interestingly cylindrical beakers, which they claimed were not a typical Venetian style. When the matter was taken to court Salter was found not to be at fault, but he was apparently pressurised to lease his Winchester House furnace to Robson, who took over its running.

This was a short-lived victory for Robson who, up until this point had only attempted to exploit the crystal or Venetian-style niche. In the meantime immigrant glassmakers continued to dominate the green glass vessel and window-glass markets. In particular, Bungar was still operating in the Weald and producing significant quantities of window glass for London consumers. To break this hold over the market, Robson bought the patent rights that had been secured by Sir Roger Aston in 1606 to make green and window glass in Ireland that, as Aston had never taken these up, had become dormant.

It was becoming increasingly apparent to many in the early seventeenth century that the decimation of woodland areas by the glass industry, among others, could not be sustained. The first manifestation of a change was when in July 1610 Sir William Slingsby was awarded a new patent to make erect furnaces for 'refining and melting glass' using 'sea-coal and pit coal'. It would appear that Slingsby never had time to exploit this patent because in the subsequent year a more serious challenge arose.

In 1611 a company was formed by Sir Edward Zouch, Thomas Mefflyn, Bevis Thelwell and Thomas Percival. They obtained a patent to make glass by using coal and, unlike Slingsby, acted quickly, immediately producing window glass and, by September 1612, clear Venetian-style glasses as well. What ensued was a messy wrangle between Robson and Zouch, with various appeals and counter-appeals first to the privy council and then ultimately the king. The final outcome was not reached until 4 March 1613/14, when all previous patents were revoked and Zouch's company was granted exclusive rights to produce any and every type of glass using coal as a fuel. The obvious attraction to the Crown was not only the preservation of the diminishing woodlands, but also the £1,000 Zouch's company had to pay annually for the privilege. This monopoly was given final and full support on 23 May 1615 with the Royal Proclamation Touching Glasses, which completely banned the use of wood as a fuel, although in practice some glassmakers could continue to gain limited concessions to do so. Against this background Robson was forced to shut his Blackfriars glasshouse in October 1614.

While considerable documentary evidence survives for theses events, particularly with regard to Robson, Salter and Zouch's enterprises in London, there is virtually no archaeological data to match it. Neither of the furnaces at Blackfriars or Winchester House have been found or excavated and it is impossible to directly identify what they produced. Robert Charleston suggested that cylindrical beakers with decorative rigaree bands and trails (59), for example, might be linked with Salter's activities, but this form is known to date to before the operating life of the Winchester House furnace, and telling domestically produced from imported designs is not possible.

The Mansell Monopoly

At the start of 1615 Zouch's company was expanded by nine members and there was a reaffirmation of the patent. One of these new people was Sir Robert Mansell and within the year he had bought out his other company partners to gain the sole control of the industry, the first time any single person had achieved this. Straight away he concentrated his efforts in two areas; both window and vessel-glass production.

The Window-Glass Market

Prior to Mansell's takeover of the monopoly, production of window glass in the south of the country was still dominated by Bungar. However, there appears to have been a shortage of window glass at this time, as in April 1617 the Glazier's Company

59 Cylindrical beakers from London. *Author*

complained to the privy council about the lack of available glass on the market. This was a situation that at first Mansell was in no position to remedy, and after the Glazier's Company's complaint Bungar was sanctioned by the privy council to continue his Wealden production using wood for fuel until 1618.

It was clear that Mansell needed to establish new window-glass furnaces and rapidly. His first attempt was at Kimmeridge Bay in Dorset, where a furnace was built on land leased from Sir William Clavell who had previously, and unsuccessfully, tried to manufacture alum here. The location was, on the face of it, an attractive one as Clavell had already built a substantial stone pier, the remains of which are still visible today, suitable for the mooring of quite large ships, and the bay itself was a natural source of oil shale that it was hoped to use as a suitable fuel for glassmaking. However, this first attempt at glassmaking at Kimmeridge rapidly proved to be abortive, as it was recorded that 'the cole proved altogether unuseful' and Mansell had no option but to recall his glassmakers before successful production could be achieved. The precise location of this furnace is unknown, but it is likely that is was close by to the second one built at the site a few years later.

Other attempts to establish new furnaces in the first years of Mansell's monopoly proved to be more successful, often in collaboration with other entrepreneurs. Clearly other people outside of Mansell's company viewed glassmaking as a possible source of profitable income, and one such man was Sir Francis Willoughby. A fascinating archive covering all aspects of the Willoughby estate at Wollaton, Nottinghamshire still survives and provides a valuable record of the attempts to establish a new manufacturing base here.

The motivation for Willoughby appears to have been his numerous financial difficulties, for which his agent Robert Fosbrooke first came up with a solution on 15 June 1615 when he suggested:

The hopefull helpes and likelie means to produce theis effectes (the relief of Willoughby's debts) deo non obstante are your colemynes and misterie of glassemakinge. God Hasten the convoye of them bothe within your lordship of Wollerton…Att this present there is come downe a proclamacion prohibiting the making of any more glasse with wood; by the which I conjecture a likelihood of the re-establishing of the former commision and so by consequence a hopefull meane to settle some workes therof within your lordship here.

One interesting aspect of this statement was Fosbrooke's realisation that, with the Royal proclamation banning the use of wood in glassmaking, there was an emerging gap in the market. This potentially had a double advantage to Willoughby; not only could he profit from the manufacture of glass, but he could also use his own reserves of coal to do so. Fosbrooke does not mention whether he was aware of Mansell's monopoly for coal-fired glass production, but it is clear that Sir Percival Willoughby leapt at this suggestion.

There is a surviving illustration in Willoughby's own hand that was drawn up just fifteen days after Fosbrooke's letter (60). It is the ground plan for the proposed glasshouse and appears to be a fanciful depiction of what Willoughby thought a glasshouse should look like, rather than reflecting any feasible design. It shows a very schematic layout with an attached dwelling, although the actual details of the furnace are virtually absent. This design was almost certainly never built and, by 8 December 1615, it is recorded that Willoughby was already concluding an agreement whereby he rented out to Mansell the great barn at Wollaton, a house, a garden and other buildings formerly used for malting for the establishment of a furnace.

This document also mentioned for the first time two glassmakers: Jacob Henzey (clearly of the already established Huguenot family) and John Squire (who was probably the same man as John Esquire recorded at Bishops Wood, Staffordshire just over a decade before). It was also agreed that Willoughby would supply as much coal as the workers wanted 'to use in two glass works lately erected at the said barn'. The estate archive also contains other papers relating to the operation of the furnace, and particularly interesting is the anticipated levels of output of window glass from the works. The agent Fosbrooke suggested that, on the basis that a case of window glass was a horse load and that ten cases would weigh a ton, two good workmen could make around sixteen to eighteen cases a week, or nearly 1.5 to 2 tons of window glass a week. On the face of it this seems an impossibly high amount, but the term 'ton' was a more flexible one in the seventeenth century, and often based on volume not weight. It either equated to a large barrel of liquid or, and more probably in this case, was taken to be the same volume as 40 cubic feet of timber. This still seems a large amount, unless of course this volume also included the generous packing that the glass would require for its safe transport.

There are other interesting documents and these include details of shipping costs and potential markets for the glass. It is clear that, despite the distance, London was still seen as the primary market, albeit via a three-step process that saw the glass moved from Wollaton to the Trent where it was barged to Hull and then put on ship for the capital, at a total cost of 1l 2s 7d per ton.

Whether the real level of output matched that initially anticipated is uncertain. Further documents indicated that the two furnaces were working for different purposes: one for 'broadglasse' or windows and the other for 'greene glasse' or vessels. However, there were clearly problems with the enterprise, even if these were not explicitly stated. For example, after 1617 there are no surviving records that refer to the glasshouse, and this probably represents a cessation of production. In 1624 Mansell himself admitted having erected a works 'on the Trent' without long-term success and a proposal was made to

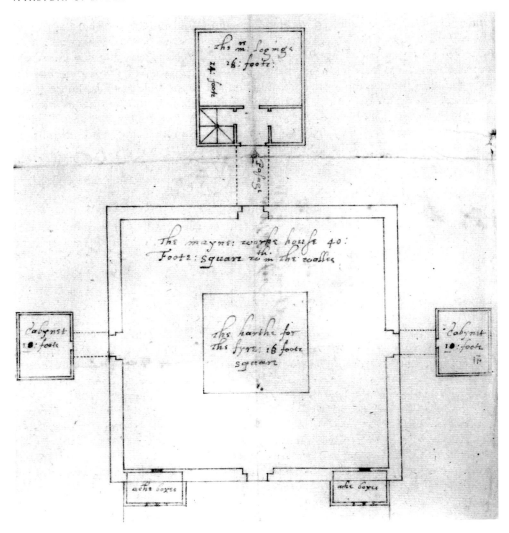

60 Sir Percival Willoughby's plan for a furnace at Wollaton, 1615. *Manuscripts and Special Collections, The University of Nottingham Mi 5 165/130*

construct another glasshouse at Awsworth only a few miles to the north-west. Again, it is unknown whether this second Nottinghamshire enterprise was successful, but an estate map of New Awsworth in 1690 shows the location of a glasshouse, and Houghton's list of 1696 (discussed in chapter five) records two glasshouses in the vicinity. Whether any of these later works had their origins in the Mansell monopoly is less certain.

Mansell's other, and ultimately much more successful, expansion of window glass manufacture took place at Newcastle upon Tyne from the end of 1617 onwards. The first indication that glassmakers were in the area occurs in February 1617/18 when it was recorded that 'Edward Henzey servant to Sir Robert Mannsfield' was buried at All Saints' church. Certainly by April 1618 it is apparent that the Newcastle furnaces were up and running successfully and initial disruption among the workers, fermented by

Bungar himself, were quashed by the appointment of William Robson, once the rival of Mansell, as manager. Glass was produced in large quantities at Newcastle, around 3,000-4,000 cases per year, and shipped on the same barges as coal down the East Coast and into London. The precise location of these earliest Tyneside works is not known, but it is likely that they were on the north bank at Byker, and it is possible that Glasshouse Street, which appears on the map today, might provide a rough indication of their location.

With Newcastle successfully supplying the window glass to London and the East Coast, other sources were required for the rest of the country, although unfortunately rather less is known about these. In 1624 Mansell himself claimed that he had built nine other broad-glass furnaces for the purposes of supplying this demand. The locations of most of these are unknown, but at around this time Paul Tyzack became established at Stourbridge and Francis Bristow at Coventry, presumably both under licence from Mansell. Indeed, it is clear that Mansell continued to expand his provision of window-glass production; as late as 1631 he built a new furnace on grounds leased from the Earl of Strafford at Wentworth in South Yorkshire, to be run by the same Francis Bristow who had had previously worked at Coventry.

Mansell's Expansion of Production in London

While window production might have been the most immediate of Mansell's concerns, it was not long until he involved himself with vessel production. Despite his establishment of a furnace at Wollaton, Nottinghamshire, which was making green vessel glass, this was the only one in operation at the start of his monopoly and it is hardly surprising that, by 1615/16, such a shortage of vessel glass of all kinds had occurred in London that merchants were importing it from the Continent in breach of the monopoly.

Mansell had to (and did) respond by providing two new London furnaces. The first was built at Ratcliffe in 1616 for the production of green glasses, and was leased to a group of merchants fronted by Thomas Robinson for an annual rent of £300. It was later claimed by Mansell's attorney that the cost of building this furnace was £300, but little more is known of its form or precise location. Its output is also unclear; drinking glasses are assumed to be its main output, but it was also stated in March 1620 that it was making hourglass phials, suggesting that pharmaceutical wares were a staple product.

The second furnace built in London was constructed at the site of the old Austin Friars, Broad Street, either in 1616 or 1617. Unlike the Ratcliffe works, this was one intended to make 'crystal' or good-quality clear drinking glasses, and Mansell took a more direct interest in its operation, even residing close by. He initially hired William Robson (who had successfully operated the Blackfriars furnace) to run the operation, which was staffed with Venetians, until he was sent to manage the Newcastle window-glass furnaces in 1618. Robson was replaced by a Welshman, James Howell, who later became a more famous literary figure and who seemed to know little of glassmaking and, in turn, was replaced by Captain Francis Bacon, an old naval companion of Mansell.

Of the furnace itself again rather little is known. No surviving remains have been found, and its precise location in the Austin Friars complex on Broad Street is uncertain. However, unlike the Ratcliffe furnace, through historical and archaeological sources its products can be more easily identified. In both 1624 and 1635 Mansell published price lists for his products and these also referred to the earlier costs of 1621 (*61*). These are informative for several reasons. Firstly, it is clear that Mansell was trying to demonstrate that his glasses were actually getting cheaper through time, a way of justifying his monopoly and countering growing criticism. It also shows that he was producing a variety of different types of vessels in two grades of glass; mentioning to 'crystal' and 'ordinary'. However, it is clear from the 1635 document that he was only referring to glass made at Broad Street and not the green glasses of Ratcliffe and elsewhere. It is also possible to get an impression of the forms produced, with these including beer glasses and wine glasses as well as less well-defined smaller 'crystal glasses', and 'mortars'. The inclusion of mirror-plates is also interesting, as this implies a more specialised manufacture.

	1621	1624	1635
large ordinary glasses (for beer)	6s – 7s 4d	4s 6d	4s
small ordinary glasses (for wine)	4s	2s 6d	2s 6d
crystal beer glasses	18s	15s	9s
crystal wine glasses	16s	12s	5s 6d – 7s
smallest crystal glasses	12s	10s	–
looking-glass plates	11s	8s – 10s	–
mortar glasses	2s 6d	1s 3d	1s 4d

61 Mansell's price list for his glasses (per dozen). *Adapted from Godfrey*

This range of glass types can be broadly confirmed from finds on English sites of the period, which include a range of beakers, goblets and other forms. However, until recently it has only been possible to speculatively link these archaeological vessels with Mansell. This changed in 1990 when excavations close to Broad Street revealed the remains of the city ditch. This had been backfilled in various stages during the 1620s and 1630s to allow for the expansion of the city, and one of these dumps included a large quantity of glassmaking waste that must have derived from Mansell's nearby Broad Street furnace. This both confirmed and complicated the picture presented by the documentary evidence.

Among the glassmaking debris were various elements of waste, such as moils and paraison ends, that clearly derived from the manufacture of goblets. These were in a high-quality soda-rich glass and were probably what Mansell referred to as 'crystal' glass. Half-finished wasters suggested that goblets with cigar-shaped and mould-blown stems were made (*62a*) and sections of ribbed tubing are probably the waste from making wine glasses with serpentine stems (*62b*). It was also possible to identify some beaker and goblet forms, especially those decorated with distinctive opaque white rods, both through unfinished examples and working waste, such as paraison ends, decorated with rods (*62c*). But among the assemblage was a second type of glass, green-tinted in colour and with higher potash contents, suggesting that other local alkali sources were used. This glass, which may well represent Mansell's 'ordinary' glass, was used to make beakers (*62d*), but there were also fragments of small bottles and other items not included in his price lists. There is, however, no evidence for mirror-plates at Broad Street in the archaeological material.

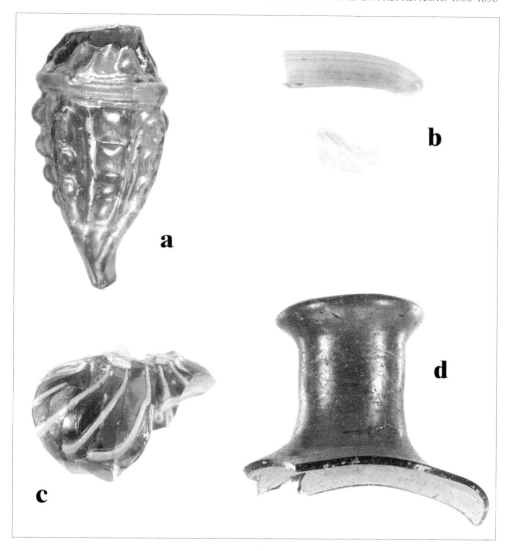

62 Glassmaking waste from Mansell's furnace on Broad Street, London. *Author*

Expansion of Vessel-Glass Manufacture Outside of London

With the successful establishment of the Ratcliffe and Broad Street furnaces to supply the London and South-Eastern markets with vessel glass, Mansell sought to exploit his monopoly in other areas of the country. With an eye to the South-West he turned again to Kimmeridge Bay and the land and resources of Sir William Clavell. In November Clavell and Mansell concluded an agreement to try and produce vessel glass for sale in Dorset, Wiltshire, Hampshire, Devon and Cornwall. In an attempt to make this a more successful venture than the window-glass enterprise just two years earlier the Lorrainer Abraham Bigo was brought from London to oversee production. It appears that, at first, Bigo started to reuse the old furnace originally intended for window-glass production but, by February 1617/18, he had agreed to run a new four-pot furnace on the site.

Bigo and Clavell appear to have put some considerable effort into making this venture a success. Indeed, it is clear they overcame the earlier technical difficulties of producing glass using oil shale, although there are some suggestions that the contemporary audience was not impressed with the overall quality of the glass. In 1625, just two years after the furnace was shut, John Crase of Puddletown described the stock of the furnace as 'only green glass of very small value'. The quality of the glass was not the only problem faced by Clavell; there may not have been the ready market for his wares that had originally been anticipated. He clearly had to push its retail widely, and there are records of sales in Dorchester, Dartmouth and elsewhere. Despite many difficulties, the furnace continued in operation until 1623, and therefore was not strictly a commercial failure, although it was always dogged by trouble. In this period between 1618-23 there were frequent references to Bigo and Clavell not paying rent to Mansell's monopoly. However, the real problem lay in where the glass could be sold, and Clavell appears to constantly have been in breach of his agreement to only sell it in the South-West. As early as 1619 there were complaints that it was being sold in London, and similar records suggest that this was still the case in 1623 when matters came to a head and the privy council was petitioned to end Clavell's sales in the capital. After being temporarily imprisoned for this infringement, Clavell continued to refuse demands that he re-enter into the original monopoly agreement with Mansell, and finally the privy council was forced to rule that the Kimmeridge furnace be demolished.

Evidence for Clavell's industrial activities were initially investigated by David Brachi in the 1970s, who found the remains of salt boiling and briquetage, as well as one of Clavell's earlier alum furnaces. In the same area, two distinct patches of glass were observed falling out of the eroding cliff edge, and a magnetic survey indicated that a furnace structure lay close to the cliff edge. Given its precarious situation excavations were undertaken by David Crossley in 1980-81 to record the furnace and identify which period of glassmaking it belonged to.

The excavations revealed one of the best-preserved glass furnaces thus far found in England (*colour plate 19*). The main furnace was of the now well-established 'wing' form. The central sieges were mainly constructed from locally occurring sandstone and clay, and clearly were intended to hold two pots each, confirming the documentary sources (*63*). Of similar construction were the four attached wings although, as with other furnaces of this design, their exact functions were not clear. However, the most distinctive feature was the very deep-running stone-flagged flue that was accessed at either end by two sets of stone steps, presumably to allow access to clear the ash created from the burning of the oil shale (*64*). The rest of the superstructure of the furnace did not survive, although there were scatters of disturbed bricks that had glass splashed on them, suggesting they were used to some extent in the furnace construction. What was also well preserved was the building in which the furnace was contained. The base courses of a stone wall survived on all sides and there were a series of post holes that probably acted as roof supports. It is perhaps unfortunate, however, that, given the preservation of the site, the wider area around the furnace was not subject to investigation, so that any ancillary features of structures were revealed.

A large quantity of crucibles and glass waste were also found. Although green tinted in colour, the glass was not as bad as might have been expected, given the somewhat derogatory contemporary comments made about it; indeed, a wide range of well-made forms were present, including small bottles, pedestal beakers, jugs and bowls. Also interesting was that a number of the crucibles appeared unused, and these were made from local Purbeck clays, two even having maker's marks on the rims. A single piece of folded iron tubing was also recovered, perhaps a portion of one of Bigo's blowing irons.

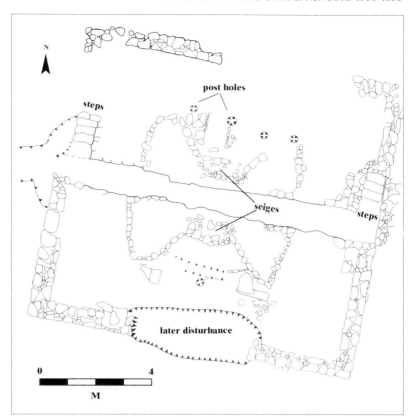

63 Plan of
the furnace at
Kimmeridge.
After Crossley

64 Steps leading into the flue at Kimmeridge. *D. Crossley*

The final glassmaking area for which there is both documentary and archaeological evidence for the production of vessel glass during the Mansell monopoly is at Haughton Green, Denton, to the south-east of Manchester. The earliest evidence for glassmaking came from the Hyde parish record when in January 1614/15 Isaac, son of Robert Hartley, glassmaker, was baptised. The following year on 8 September the daughter of Isaac de Houx was baptised in the same church, and from this time on there are occasional records of immigrant glassmakers from the de Houx and Pilmey families. It is possible that these glassmakers had come directly to Haughton Green from Bickerstaffe in 1600, although the fifteen-year gap in any documentation argues against any direct transition.

It is clear that from at least 1621 Isaac de Houx was the chief glassmaker at Haughton Green and that he was working under a leasing agreement with Mansell. Unfortunately the precise arrangements for this are not recorded, but it was probably on similar terms to that of Bigo and Clavell, to supply vessel glass to a specified area in the North-West. How long the furnace was in operation is less clear, but it probably did not survive the Civil War, which particularly affected this area. Certainly there are no records of glassmakers in the parish records after 1653, and it is known that at least some had moved to start operations in South Yorkshire.

The actual site of the furnace was first positively identified in 1968 to the north of Haughton Green at Glass House Fold and by the site of a later coal pit, the debris of which covered the area. The site was partially excavated between 1969-73 by the Pilkington Glass Museum under the direction of Ruth Hurst Vose. The main aim was to uncover and completely remove for permanent display the main furnace structure, which unfortunately left fewer resources for the investigation of the surrounding area and features. The main furnace, located in the northern area of the excavation, was found to be a in a good state of preservation (65). Constructed from sandstone blocks, it did differ from other immigrant-style furnaces, not having the familiar attached wings.

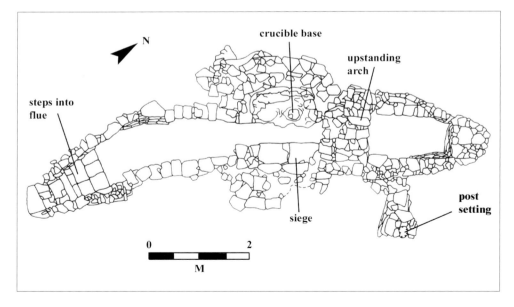

65 Plan of the main furnace at Haughton Green. *After Hurst-Vose*

The excavator described the furnace as being banana-shaped, although it really was rectangular in form with large extending flues, one of which was curved. The main melting area of the furnace was around 3m square with two internal siege benches, one of which had the fused remains of two crucible bases in situ. The flue, being similar to Kimmeridge, was also deep and stone flagged, although only accessed by a single set of stone steps. More importantly, at the point where the flue left the main melting chamber, portions of its barrel-vaulted roof survived intact, the apex of which stood 1.2m above the flue base, leaving ample space for access. The last interesting feature was a posthole surrounded by a stone setting, attached to the furnace on its north-eastern side, but out of the way from the working area. The function of this single posthole was unclear, there being no others that would suggest the presence of a roof, and the excavator's interpretation that this was to hold a small hoist to help lower new pots into the furnace seems plausible.

To the south of the main furnace were a series of three subsidiary rectangular ovens, two formed from an internal partition and the third, perhaps built a little later, adjoining them (66). These had internal diameters of around 1.75m x 2m, and again were constructed from sandstone blocks and with flagged floors. All three had evidence for internal burning, but the lack of flues suggests that they were not intended for prolonged heating. Perhaps the most likely explanation was that they were used in a similar way to a bread oven, where a fire was lit to heat the chamber and once this was hot the embers raked out so items could be placed inside. If this were the case then it would appear that these were annealing ovens, heated to a reasonable temperature, but then allowed to cool slowly with the finished glasses inside.

As might be expected, a significant quantity of crucibles, waste and vessel glass was found during the course of the excavations. The majority were very similar to other contemporary sites, green in colour and of a good quality. Products included a range of small bottles, pedestal beakers, jugs and even bowls. However, what was more unusual

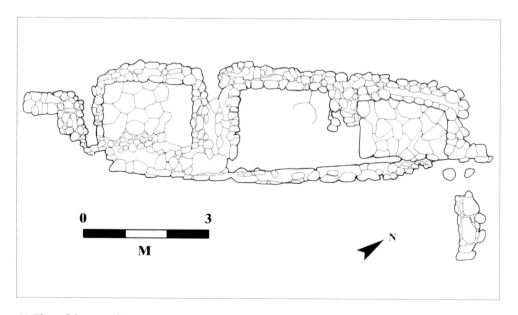

66 Plan of the annealing ovens at Haughton Green. *After Hurst-Vose*

was that deliberately coloured glass was also being made, albeit in small quantities. Some of this was a black, or more precisely a very dark amber, glass and formed around ten per cent of the total assemblage. Black glass was used to make a similar range of beakers, bottles and jugs to the green glass. The other colour present was a light-blue glass, which only made up two per cent of the total found, and despite this small quantity it is still possible to identify jugs and bowls as vessels made in this colour. Interestingly the site was also making window glass, using the cylinder method.

Other items of interest found on the site include the crucibles. These were mainly of the standard straight-sided bucket-shaped form. However, a few did have rims that seemed to suggest that they had a v-shaped section cut out of them. This, together with the find of a single flat disc made in a crucible clay, has led to the assertion that at least some of the crucibles had lids, and access to the batch inside was through the small cut opening. If true this is interesting, as it would constitute the first use of covered pots. It is often stated that to stop the coal fumes affecting the quality of any glass being melted, a covered crucible was required, although there is rather less actual evidence for this. Certainly by the early eighteenth century closed crucibles were being used for the production of glass at some sites, but this was in connection with the making of high-quality and colourless lead glasses. Whether a closed crucible would really have been necessary for the production of ordinary green, black and blue glass at Haughton Green is rather less certain.

Crisis in the Industry

With his establishment of new furnaces in London and his leasing of production rights to subsidiary partners, Mansell's command of his monopoly was established and seemingly unassailable. This is not to say there were not attempts by others to challenge his monopoly rights. For example, in 1621 Bungar, this time with the aid of John Worrall, a drinking glassmaker trained by Robson at Blackfriars, unsuccessfully petitioned the privy council that other Englishmen should be allowed to make glass. Later in the same year the Commons also sought to suppress a number of patents, including that pertaining to glass, but in this instance the king was not inclined to agree.

Mansell was then in a position to seek a new revision of the patent. He claimed that the excessively high rent he had to pay to the Crown made it impossible for him to compete in price with glass made both on the Continent and in Scotland. The privy council therefore formed a committee of four Glass Commissioners on 12 October 1622 to look into the matter. Their report recommended that a new patent be issued to Mansell alone, as opposed to the company of nine that were technically still in receipt of the old one, that wood should still be banned as fuel and that Mansell should pay no rent to the Crown. However, this easing in rent was to be balanced by the fact that glass could be freely imported from abroad subject to an imposition through which the king could make up the lost revenue. This was actually a masterful solution; the greatest criticism against Mansell's monopoly had been from merchants and glaziers who had complained about a lack of glass, and they could now import this freely from abroad. Mansell himself faced lower overheads, but the threat of foreign competition would ensure he still kept his prices low, and the Crown still generated its revenue. The new patent was granted on 22 May 1623 and set to expire in 1638.

With this new revised patent, there was little further opposition to Mansell. The ordered destruction of Clavell's Kimmeridge glasshouse in 1623 demonstrated that Mansell's rights would be enforced and, although Bungar continued for some years to try and cause trouble, primarily through a series of printed pamphlets, this little affected the business. The amount of vessel glass that was being imported seems to have been relatively low, again not having a serious impact on Mansell. That was until 1630, when one of Mansell's chief clerks, a man called Vecon, stole off to France with a considerable sum of Mansell's money. Using this, Vecon established a furnace on the French coast with the express intention of producing glass for the English market. To add insult to injury he even managed to poach a number of Mansell's Italian workers from Broad Street. Soon a large quantity of glass was reaching England and Mansell petitioned, and was granted on 25 June 1630, a revision of his patent banning the importation of drinking glasses and mirrors, unless they were from Venice herself.

Mansell's handling of the glass industry in the 1630s continued to be successful. Production clearly increased and he was even granted on 1 March 1634/5 an extension to his monopoly rights to cover Ireland for the rent of £1,500. But matters outside of his control abruptly ended his years of hard work. The steadily deteriorating political situation saw the Scots invade northern England and they reached Newcastle in the summer of 1640. The approach of the army caused his workmen to flee from Newcastle, glass already made could not be shipped and most importantly the supply of coal from Newcastle, so vital for his London furnaces, ceased.

The cessation of production in London caused an immediate shortage of glass and, perhaps sensing that Mansell's position was waning, there were renewed challenges to his patent in 1641, although these were never properly heard by a rather preoccupied parliament. Indeed, by 1642, with the Commons now in open opposition to the king, Mansell was ordered to surrender his Royal patent on 30 May, just two months before armed conflict broke out.

At first Mansell was still able to continue his industrial activities. Being too old to take an active part in the hostilities, he restored works at Newcastle in 1645 once the Scottish army had withdrawn. But without a monopoly his competitors were able to challenge him, and two new glasshouses were built in Newcastle and successfully run by a Mr Harris. Mansell finally died in 1656 aged eighty-three and his Newcastle furnaces were taken over by the Tyzacks and Henseys who had been working there. It is less certain what happened to the Broad Street furnace, and although it possibly continued production through the 1650s it is unlikely to have survived long. Certainly the styles and types of high-quality glassware that was popular from the 1620-40s fell out of fashion, and the overall use of drinking glasses was in decline throughout the period of the Commonwealth. Therefore, despite Mansell's forty-one-year involvement, a time when he founded it as a viable and successful business across the country, it was to be others who were finally to establish England's place as a world leader in the industry.

5

SCIENTISTS AND INDUSTRIALISTS 1650-1800

With the onset of civil war and the cancellation of Mansell's monopoly, the state of the industry in the years immediately following is hard to ascertain for certain. It is clear that glass production continued throughout this period. For instance, Mansell continued to run his Newcastle works until his death in 1656, while the Henzey and Tyzack families were operating in and around Stourbridge. However, without the formal regulation of a monopoly system it is hard to assess the level or extent of the industry. In all likelihood production only continued on a relatively small scale.

The Commonwealth

Robert Charleston, among others, suggested that the Puritan government of the interregnum might have disapproved of the use of drinking glasses, and this would have reduced demand. There is little evidence for this, and there certainly would have been a continuing requirement for windows. Perhaps the real reason for the possible decline in production was the financial hardship brought on by war, which would have certainly affected the demand for luxury goods. Yet this was also a time where new innovative forms of glassware were being developed and rapidly adopted in the country. The classic English wine bottle, the earliest form of which is the so-called shaft and globe (*67*), was first produced in the 1640s-1650s and this rapidly became the most common piece of domestic glassware within a couple of decades.

There are documentary sources indicating that there was a continuing demand for glass during the interregnum. Surviving from 1657 is the *Book of Rates* that listed the taxable rates of goods arriving in London (*68*). Although it provides no indication on the quantities that were being imported, it demonstrates the range of items thought worthy of taxation, and these are fairly detailed. For example, window glass was mentioned as being primarily from three sources: Burgundy, Normandy and Rhenish, while window glass of inferior quality was described as Muscovia glass, although whether this came from Russia is less certain.

While precise types are not specified, drinking glasses were noted as coming from Venice, Flanders and France. From the rates charged those of Venetian origin were considered best, and those from Flanders were superior to the French ones. Other glasses listed were of less certain forms. The 'burning glasses' might have been magnifying glasses

67 Shaft and globe wine bottle,
*c.*1650. *Author*

or lenses, while 'balm glasses' and 'vials' were probably small medicinal bottles. The last two types mentioned were 'water glasses', an uncertain form, and 'hour-glasses'.

From this brief outline in the 1657 *Book of Rates* it is possible to gain an impression of the ranges of vessels and variety of window glass in demand at this time. However, what is less certain is what, if any, of this demand was actually met by domestic production. Archaeologically, there is virtually no evidence for furnaces operating at this time, the one possible exception might be Haughton Green, where production is suggested to have continued until 1653. Of the furnaces run by Mansell in Newcastle, there is no surviving evidence, and to date no production site belonging to this period has been identified elsewhere in England. Indeed, it is only with the Restoration in 1660 that more information on the glass industry emerges.

Production and the Glass Trade in London

Although the return of the monarchy provided new opportunities for industrial entrepreneurs, the climate was different to the one preceding the Civil War, and it was never again possible for a single individual to dominate the industry. Charles II never reintroduced such a system of rigid monopolies and patents, in part due to the fact that these had led to a great deal of resentment against his father and accusations of favouritism. However, another reason that a single individual never rose to dominate the glass industry was partly due to the fact that it was to expand so rapidly during the latter half of the seventeenth century, and in new diverse ways, so that no one person could fully control it.

One change that did come about with the Restoration was the establishment of the Worshipful Company of Glass Sellers. There had been an early attempt to form one in 1635, with a charter obtained from Charles I; however, the City of London refused to enrol it. It was proposed that the company would act in a similar way to the already existing Glaziers Company, by operating a retail monopoly for all glass tableware, mirrors, hourglasses and all categories other than window glass and spectacles. Four years after the return of the king, on 25 July 1664, a Royal Charter was finally granted to the Company of Glass Sellers, and this was enrolled on 28 September. This gave the company a constitution and a governing body that was empowered to maintain and enforce standards, levy fines on glassmakers should they break regulations and, more significantly, control the trade of glass, particularly that undertaken by journeymen and hawkers.

However, as it grew in standing and confidence, the company started to make attempts to gain prohibitions against imported glass. For instance, in 1669 there was an unsuccessful attempt to limit the importation of Venetian mirror plates. Just a year later similar attempts were made to ban the importation of vessel glass, when on the 24 November a petition 'agreed that the company do endeavour to obtain a prohibition' on all foreign drinking glasses. However, this too seems to have been unsuccessful, and clearly the main stumbling block was that for any importation ban to even be considered there had to be a sufficient supply of domestically produced glass to fill the gap, and this was clearly not the case in the years around 1670.

The newly established Glass Sellers Company was not the only party to benefit from the Restoration; other individuals were also quick to see the potential business opportunities with the return of the monarchy. The most influential of these was George Villiers, the 2nd Duke of Buckingham, one of the richest men in England and a favoured courtier of Charles II. Just three months after Charles' return, on 18 August 1660, Buckingham made an agreement with the French glassmaker John de la Cam. He was to provide de la Cam with land at Charterhouse Yard in London and the sum of £6,000 to build and run a glasshouse. In return de la Cam was to make 'cristall de roach or Venice cristall' for up to ten years. Buckingham also sought to obtain a patent from the king to protect his new business and, although it is not recorded whether he was successful in this request, it is likely that Charles would have looked favourably on the suggestion. Interestingly, and with echoes to the preceding century, one condition placed on de la Cam was that he was to also teach the art of glassmaking to Buckingham's own men.

Despite this considerable investment by Buckingham, de la Cam did not remain for the ten agreed years, leaving England late in 1661, although the precise reason for this is uncertain. He later became master of the glasshouse at Nijmegen, making this the first of several glassmaking connections between the two towns. In the absence of de la Cam a licence was issued to Martin Clifford and Thomas Paulden for the making of crystal glass for fourteen years. Clifford was an old companion of Buckingham and not a glassmaker by profession. Paulden is less well documented, but it seems probable he must have been a trained glassmaker to make the issued licence viable. Early in 1663 Buckingham was granted a patent to make crystal glass and on 4 August this was extended to mirrors too, although with the condition that the merchant Thomas Tilson be granted the sole rights to sell the products for up to fourteen years. Buckingham's influence over the English glass industry was further strengthened on 25 July 1664 by a proclamation forbidding the importation of mirror-glass plates.

It is also interesting to look at the rates being charged on imported glass at the start of Charles II's reign. With his return in 1660 and just three years after the surviving Commonwealth port book, significant variations in the level of duty imposed on imported glass can be observed (68). With the exceptions of the white (or clear) Normandy and Muscovia glass, all the window imports show a dramatic rise in duty rates. The reasons for this are unclear, but one possible explanation might be that as early as 1660 the Crown was hoping to protect and stimulate the domestic window glass industry that, although largely unrecorded, was apparently still operating in a variety of locations. The picture is a little more complex for drinking glasses. There was again a significant rise in duty on Venetian glass, but a sizable decrease in duty on Flanders and French glass. The fact that duty was actually lowered on drinking glasses from nearby continental sources indicates that there was little or no native production, a situation that would explain Buckingham's very early interest in the establishment of a new furnace at Charterhouse. Most other glass types saw more moderate rises in duty, the exceptions being burning and balm glasses, although the reason for their decrease is less certain. Finally some new types of glassware, such as 'pipes' were mentioned, but what these actually were is still unclear.

Item		1657	1660
Glass for windows	Burgundy white, the chest or case	1 10 0	3 15 0
	Burgundy coloured, the chest	1 10 0	5 5 0
	Normandy white, the case	1 10 0	1 10 0
	Normandy coloured, the case	1 10 0	3 15 0
	Rhenish, the way containing 60 bunches	1 10 0	4 10 0
	Muscovia glass or slude, the pound	0 2 0	0 2 0
Drinking glasses called	Venice drinking glasses, the dozen	0 4 3	0 18 0
	Flanders drinking glasses, the hundred	2 10 0	1 5 0
	French drinking glasses, the hundred	1 10 0	0 15 0
	Course drinking the dozen	–	0 3 0
Glasses called	Burning glasses, the dozen	0 12 0	0 3 0
	Balm glasses, the groce	2 0 0	0 7 6
	Vials, the hundred	0 10 0	0 15 0
	Water glasses of all sorts, the dozen	0 3 0	0 12 0

		1657	1660
Looking glasses	Penny ware, the groce	-	0 16 0
	Halfe penny ware, the groce	0 6 8	0 8 0
Hour-glasses	of Flanders making, course, the groce	2 0 0	3 0 0
	of Flanders making, the dozen, fine	-	1 0 0
	of Venise making the dozen	2 0 0	3 0 0
Glass pipes	Glasse pipes, small, the pound	-	0 7 6
	Glasse pipes, great, cwt	-	7 10 0

68 Excise levied on glass listed in the books of rates for 1657 and 1660. *Adapted from Godfrey*

The rate books, as well as the record of Buckingham's enterprises, give a general picture of production in the early years after the Civil War. There appears to have been some, as yet unquantifiable, level of window-glass production taking place and the same is probably also true for other green glasses, such as bottles. However, in terms of more specialist wares such as fine drinking vessels and mirror glass, production appears to have ceased during the interregnum.

As part of Buckingham's attempt to revive the more specialised aspects of English glassmaking, he established a second furnace at Vauxhall. While Charterhouse was intended for vessel-glass production, the new Vauxhall site was specifically for mirror plates. The precise year it opened is a matter of some debate. It was certainly some time before 1671, and most likely the factory was founded in 1664, the year that the Royal proclamation banned the import of Venetian-made mirror plates. Despite the slight ambiguity of its establishment, it is known that between March 1671 and April 1674 the Vauxhall furnace was run by John Bellingham. He was already a recognised mirror specialist and had worked in the industry since at least 1666 in both Haarlem and Amsterdam.

The mirror-plate furnace at Vauxhall seems to have been in some significant financial difficulties as early as 1674 and, shortly after, Buckingham was forced to relinquish much of his control in the venture to George Ravenscroft. In his attempt to turn around the fortunes of the works, Ravenscroft employed a Benjamin Baker, who was already experienced in mirror-plate manufacture, and this caused an understandably angry reaction from Bellingham. However, Ravenscroft's administration seems to have turned around the fortunes of the furnace, and it continued for many decades to produce plate glass. Although the precise timing is uncertain, it appears that during 1675 Buckingham completely relinquished control of the Vauxhall works, and probably the Charterhouse furnace as well, and effectively his involvement in the industry was at an end.

The diarist John Evelyn, who was also a founding member of the new Royal Society and had an interest in new technologies and industries, visited the Vauxhall works on 19 September 1676, when he recalled seeing 'huge vasas of metal as cleare and ponderous and thick as Chrystal, also looking glasses far larger and better than any from Venice'. This description confirms that Evelyn was clearly impressed by the quality of glass. While it is commonly accepted that the Charterhouse furnace was making vessel glass, Charleston and other commentators have suggested that Buckingham established a second, less well-recorded, furnace for this purpose. Again Evelyn is the source for this when, on 10 June 1673, he went 'to the Italian glasse-house at Greenewich' where he saw 'glasse blowne of finer metal than that of Muran'. There is no direct evidence that this furnace belonged to Buckingham, indeed it is strange that Evelyn describes it as the 'italian glasse-house'. On the other hand, he visited it only a year after Buckingham had been granted a patent to produce crystal glass, so it would be unlikely that it would have been allowed to operate if it had not been under his control. Nevertheless, little more is known of this works and it is impossible to say how long it might have operated.

It is unfortunate that, given this documentary evidence for the revival of the quality end of glassmaking, there is very little archaeological confirmation of this phase of the industry. Neither the early furnace at Vauxhall, nor those at Charterhouse Yard or Greenwich have been precisely located and excavated. The only very tentative evidence is some fragments of cast, but unfinished, plate glass that were found during the excavations of the slightly later furnace at Vauxhall situated across the road from Buckingham's works (69). Likewise, the archaeological record is scarce on information

69 Plate mirror glass, almost certainly manufactured at the Duke of Buckingham's Vauxhall furnace. *Author*

on what glass was actually being used in England as a whole, irrespective of where it was made here. During the 1660s-1670s finds of vessel and mirror glass in domestic contexts are fairly rare compared with fifty years earlier, and the overall picture archaeologically is that there was relatively little glass used in England at this time, let alone produced.

The lack of home production inevitably required the supply of the market from foreign sources, and this is clearly evidenced by the surviving set of eight letters from the London merchants John Greene and Michael Measey to the Venetian Allesio Morelli between October 1667 and November 1672. The full transcripts of these letters were published by Albert Hartshorne in *Old English Drinking Glass* in 1897. While it is clear that these eight letters were an in-depth record of the correspondence between the two parties, there were clearly other letters referred to that no longer survive. Nonetheless, their contents are of considerable interest. Each letter was also accompanied by a series of accurate and scaled drawings of the items that Greene and Measey were ordering, which include vessels, window plates, faux pearls and other objects. Greene and Measey were members of the Glass Sellers Company, and probably not the only merchants to be importing Venetian glass. Yet the scale of what was being ordered is impressive; in the five years that the letters span they ordered in excess of 30,000 vessels as well as large quantities of mirror plates and other items. It is clear that not all of these orders may have actually arrived, but it does indicate the scale of glass importation at a time usually thought, both historically and archaeologically, to be one of comparatively low glass usage.

The letters provide many insights into how the mechanics of the glass trade worked. For instance, in the third letter, dated 17 September 1669, Greene asks that the glass be packed into a

strong large whole chest, well hoopd and naijld and markt and numberd as in the margent at one end of eerij chest and also apone the covers and lids, to prevent the seamen from setting the lid or upper part of the chest undermost and to be very sure theij be all verij well and carefulij packt up and with thorou drij weeds, for if the weeds be not well drijd or doe take anij wett after theij be packt theij staijn and spoijle the glasses.

The packing of the glass into hooped chests is not surprising, but it is interesting to see that the chests themselves were padded with 'weeds'. Given the location of Venice, it is most likely that these were in fact seaweed, and it is not surprising that Greene was concerned that it should be dry.

Several letters contain rather vocal complaints to Morelli, often connected to the way the glass was packaged. In the second letter dated 28 August 1668, Measey and Greene complained that 'chest no.5 it was almost quite spoijled it had receveid much wett which had rotted the glasses', while some of the glasses sent were smaller than those illustrated in a previous order or made of an inferior quality of glass. Other letters hint at wider developments in the English glass industry. In the final letter sent by Greene on 30 November 1672 he concluded 'I see bij other merchants ffactorijs heer that looking glasses are now bought cheaper than latelj thej have bin.' This is perhaps a confirmation of Evelyn's observation of 1673 that the mirror glass made at Vauxhall was of a growing quality that could rival that of Venice.

Unfortunately, the illustrations that accompany the letters have never been properly studied or comprehensively published, but what is striking is the amount of repetition that occurs within them. Three broad categories can be defined, although there are other variations. The first were stemmed vessels, or goblets (*70*). The majority of these

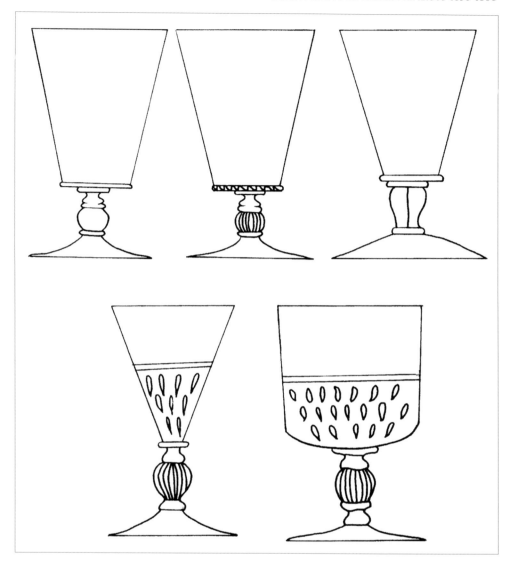

70 Some goblet types accompanying the letters of John Greene and Michael Measey. *After Hartshorne*

were characterised by plain bucket-shaped bowls, round knops that were either plain or ribbed, and indeed these are the most common goblets of the period found archaeo-logically (e.g. *colour plate 20a*). A less common variation had a vertically indented knop, caused by impressing the stem four times to produce a quatrefoil shape. Other goblet forms had either more tapered or rounded bowls, and the Greene illustrations seem to indicate that these had a moulded design, again a feature known archaeologically (*colour plate 20b*). The second general type shown was the tumbler. Unlike earlier beaker forms that were taller than they were broad, these were relatively simple and squat vessels, although often depicted in various sizes (*71*). Many were plain, but others clearly had vertical or horizontal ribbing, and some a moulded teardrop decoration, all of which are

71 Some beaker types accompanying the letters of John Greene and Michael Measey. *After Hartshorne*

forms found on excavations (*colour plate 20d*). A variation on the tumbler had two applied handles and a spout, and this form was the first appearance of the posset, designed for the drinking of hot milk curdled with ale. The final broad category of vessel consisted of those for purposes other than drinking (*72*). These included vases of various shapes, as well as double compartment cruets for oil and vinegar and lidded pots.

In addition to the illustrations, Green and Measey also included little annotations specifying colour or additional decoration such as 'eares and of goode fashions'. Interestingly a number of vessels were specified as being 'enameld' and 'speckled enameld', which may seem odd descriptions. However, a few surviving pieces are indeed decorated in this way. Recent excavations at 1 Poultry in London revealed a number of opaque white glasses with a coloured speckled decoration on their surfaces that dated to this exact period (*colour plate 20c*). What is even more interesting is that in his fourth letter to Morelli, dated 10 February 1670, Greene asks 'when you wright to mee, direct yor letter: ffor Mr. John Greene at ye Kings Armes in the Poultrij London.' While the excavated glasses from 1 Poultry could not be directly connected with either the Kings Arms or John Greene, their presence might not be purely coincidental.

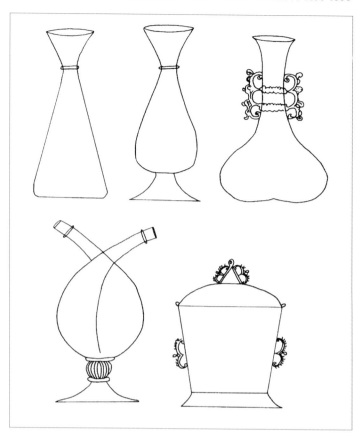

72 Other types of glass accompanying the letters of John Greene and Michael Measey. *After Hartshorne*

George Ravenscroft and the New Crystal

By 1675 the Duke of Buckingham had ceased to be involved in the glass industry and left permanent residence in London, later dying in 1685. Yet it appears that the domestic industry was in a state of revival. The possible improvement in English glassmaking was noted as early as 15 September 1673 when the Venetian secretary in London, Girolamo Alberti, remarked in a despatch home that 'two new furnaces lately opened for very fine large crystal'. An English document, dating to 1673, records that George Ravenscroft built a new glasshouse at the Savoy in London and perhaps this is one of the ones mentioned by Alberti.

George Ravenscroft is best known for the invention and development of lead crystal, one of the greatest innovations in English glassmaking. However, this accreditation is not necessarily true and requires more detailed examination. Ravenscroft came from a Catholic mercantile family and had lived and worked as his father's agent in Venice, where he had been involved in a number of industries, including glass. Therefore, it is of little surprise that Ravenscroft could see the opportunities present back home in England and sought to exploit the relatively open field of quality glass manufacture. How he became acquainted well enough with Buckingham in the first place to be asked to take over the running of the Charterhouse factory in 1673 is uncertain. However, within a year he felt secure enough to petition the king for a patent, which was granted on 16 May 1674. This patent, which was initially granted for a period of seven years, was for the production of:

a perticuler sort of christaline glasse resembling rock christall, not formerly exercised or vsed in this our kingdome, and by his greate disbursemte having so improved the same thereby to bee able to supply both inland and outland market, whereby the publique may be greatly advantaged.

Furthermore, even before this patent, Ravenscroft had secured an agreement that the Company of Glass Sellers would undertake to buy his glasses for a period of three years. Possibly in anticipation of increased demand, Ravenscroft opened another glasshouse at Henley-on-Thames and set about looking for experienced workers for both here and the Savoy factory. It is recorded that he was successful in this regard; a Venetian called Vicenzo (suggested by Charleston to be Vincenzo Pompeio) came in 1674 to work at the Savoy, while at Henley the chief glassmaker was a da Costa Montferratees, an Altarian glassmaker from northern Italy. Despite Ravenscroft's apparent competence and self-assurance, it seems that the Glass Sellers Company had less faith in him. On 13 October 1674 they wrote to him asking that a Samuel Moore might have a say in what was being made as he knew better 'what is fitter to the trade both as to ffashion and size, than any other there'.

Ravenscroft's 'new' glass, referred to in his patent of 1664, is usually assumed to be the first lead glass, although this is far from certain. The patent merely stated that it was a new type of glass and that it imitated naturally occurring rock crystal, a point again reiterated by the Venetian Alberti when he wrote, in June 1674, that the English were making glasses that were 'very white and thick'. Clearly this was a different kind of glass as the patent demanded. The question of what it was made from is potentially answered in a description in Dr Plot's *The Natural History of Oxfordshire*, published in 1676. Here he listed the original recipe as consisting of calcined crushed flints, a fine sand (the silica source) and a solution of nitre, tartar and borax (the alkali source) that had been devised by Dr Ludwell of Wadham College, Oxford. However, this initial recipe was quickly realised to be flawed, as the resulting glasses were subject to crizzling or the appearance of fine stress-cracks in the glass. Dr Plot suggests that the recipe was adjusted so that pure river pebbles were used instead and the quantity of the nitre, tartar and borax reduced.

This modified recipe seems to have produced, in the short term at any rate, a more stable glass and, as early as June 1676, newspaper adverts were being placed proclaiming that previous problems with the mixture had been solved. As a way of confirming this, Ravenscroft signed an agreement with the Glass Sellers on 29 May 1677 that he would place a glass seal stamped with a raven's head on all his glasses (73). In fact, not all glasses stamped with the raven's-head seal were free of crizzling; there are a significant number that have survived in historical collections that are heavily affected, suggesting that the revised recipe merely reduced or slowed down the appearance of fine cracks.

However, of greater interest is what was actually in the mixture and who was responsible for the so-called invention of this new crystal glass. Charleston has rightly pointed out that, although Dr Plot does not mention the presence of lead in either of the two different glasses, all glasses with a raven's head seal that have been chemically analysed have so far shown significant levels of lead oxide in their batch. This has resulted in the reasonable suggestion that lead was included, at least in the revised recipe of Ravenscroft glasses, probably in the form of minium or red lead, but that Plot was simply unaware of this. However, the degree to which Ravenscroft himself can be credited with any of these innovations is questionable. Dr Plot himself recorded that 'the invention of making glasses of stones or other materials at Henley-on-Thames lately (was) brought to England by Seignior da Costa a Montferratees and carried on by Mr Ravenscroft.' This

73 Sealed Ravenscroft glass
found in London. *C. Brain*

suggests that the innovation was that of da Costa and not Ravenscroft. Recent research
by Peter Francis has added weight to this hypothesis by pointing out that da Costa had
previously worked at the St Jacobsgasthuis in Nijmegen with two other glassmakers,
Jean Guillaume Reinier and John Odacio Formica. While da Costa subsequently left
for England, Reinier went to Sweden, where he was making lead glass by 1675, and
Formica went to Ireland, where he too received a patent and was making lead glass
by 1675. The implication that the lead glass was first invented in the Low Countries
is therefore compelling, given that three glassmakers who had previously collaborated
together in Nijmegen were, within such a short period of time, all be making lead-based
glasses elsewhere.

   Archaeologically, very little is known of either the Savoy or the Henley-on-Thames
furnaces, as no surviving remains have thus far been excavated. Of Ravenscroft's possible
output more is known. A number of sealed glasses have been found on excavations and
survive in museum collections. These vessels are characteristically thick and include
inverted baluster-stemmed goblets and possets of similar form to those ordered by
Greene. Furthermore, a tariff of glasses produced by Ravenscroft and dating to 1677
mentioned 'beer glasses ribbed and plain, clarett wine glasses of the same' as well as
'purlee glasses', 'diamond crewitts' and bottles of various capacities.

Despite the apparent success of his business and with just under three years of his patent left to run, Ravenscroft wrote to the Glass Sellers' Company to inform them that he was terminating his contract. The reason for this is unclear, but Charleston has plausibly suggested that, as a prominent Catholic, it was wise for Ravenscroft to take a lower profile during what was the climax of the 'Popish Plot' and the associated Protestant backlash. What happened in the immediate aftermath of Ravenscroft's stepping down is uncertain, but production almost certainly continued at the Savoy and at Henley. In February 1682 Hawley Bishopp concluded an agreement with the Glass Sellers' Company and took charge of the Savoy glasshouse, where he had in all probability been its manager for quite some time, Ravenscroft having resided and concentrated his efforts at Henley.

Other London Businesses

This was therefore a period that saw the expansion of the quality glass market in London, and there are often scant references to a number of other glassmakers and furnaces at this time, although often little more is known about them. John Houghton noted in 1696 that there were as many as twenty-four glasshouses in London, although not all were actually in operation. One of the earliest of these, which later became one of the best-known producers of eighteenth-century glass, was the Minories works at Whitechapel. This had been producing bottles from at least 1651, although it was taken over in 1678 by Michael Rackett, who made both bottles and crystal glass until at least 1691. The site was again offered on lease in 1699, and an advertisement of the same year stated that drinking glasses were produced there. Little more is known until 1738, when Richard Riccards was recorded as the owner and it was last mentioned in a survey of 1772.

Several other businesses that became well known in later decades had their origins in the late seventeenth and early eighteenth centuries. One such was the Whitefriars works, near the Temple. Its establishment was noted in the *London Gazette* for 1709, where it was reported that it was making all manner of tablewares in flint glass. However, just two years later in 1711, it was noted in *The Post Man* that the furnace had been forced to close, although the reason for its failure is not known. The site appears to have been used for other purposes until 1733 when a Captain Seal established a new furnace on the site. The contemporary survey of Robert Seymour commented that glassmaking was an 'art this gentleman is very famous' for, and it is probable that he had worked elsewhere in London prior to setting up at Whitefriars. The works operated under a number of different members of the Seal family until the 1760s, when it was first taken over by the Stafford and then the Holmes family. Whitefriars, however, is always inextricably linked with the company of James Powell and Sons, who bought the works in 1835 and became the most innovative and accomplished glassmakers in England, until the factory finally became economically unviable and was closed in 1980.

Another famous glasshouse of the period was the Falcon works, located close to the Blackfriars Bridge in Southwark. The first reference to it came in 1693 when it was co-owned by Francis Jackson and John Straw, but it appears to have been founded some time before then. At this time the *London Gazette* noted that the glasshouse made 'all sorts of the best and finest drinking glasses and various glasses for ornament and likewise all sorts of glass bottles'. Such endorsements were reiterated from time to time during the early seventeenth century in other newspaper articles, although it is not until the second half of the century that the actual owners were listed. The first time names appeared was in 1752 when Hughes and Winch were listed as owners, and between

1765-1780 various trade directories listed Hughes, Hall and Co. as the operators. The factory remained in continuous production into the nineteenth century when it was taken over in 1803 by Green and Pellatt, who continued to produce glass, although they soon moved the actual furnace to an adjacent site on Holland Street.

Interestingly there is also some archaeological evidence for the Falcon works, although this is still awaiting full analysis. Excavations at Hopton Street between 1994-1997 by Pre-Construct Archaeology found considerable evidence for glassworking spanning most of the eighteenth and nineteenth centuries. There was a large amount of waste glass associated with the tenures of Green and Pellatt as well as Apsley Pellatt & Co., who succeeded to the site in 1831. However, the heavily truncated remains of an earlier furnace were also revealed. Although not all was exposed, it was simple in construction with a straight central brick-lined flue and two siege benches 2.5m long. Although its precise date has not yet been ascertained it would appear to date to the early eighteenth or even late seventeenth century.

A further site where there is both historical and archaeological evidence is the Bear Gardens glasshouse that stood on Bear Alley on the Bankside. Known to have been operated by John Bowes from at least 1678, traditionally this furnace was thought to have concentrated on making crown-window glass. In 1691 Bowles assigned his interest to a stock company, and it then seems to have switched production to mirror-plate glass until at least 1726. This documentation of the Bear Gardens glasshouse has been confirmed and expanded by recent excavations undertaken between 1995-1999 by the Museum of London Archaeology Service at Benbow House, close to the known location of the furnace. Although no physical features of the glasshouse were found, as it probably lay outside of the excavation area, a significant quantity of crucibles and waste-glass fragments were found. Interestingly, they confirmed the production of plate glass (by casting), presumably taking place in the 1691-1726 phase of operations. However, they also showed that, in the earlier period, vessel glass (*colour plate 21*), as well as window glass was made, although only in an ordinary soda rather than a lead metal.

While there are documentary sources for many of the furnaces and glassmakers operating at the luxury end of the market in London, it is important to remember that there were numerous other furnaces concentrating on simpler green window or bottle glass for which no records survive. One such was the furnace at Saltpetre Bank, Whitechapel, which, under the operation of the Dallow family, was making bottles between 1678-1730, although nothing more is known of this works or its output. Likewise there are occasional archaeological finds, such as a dump of working waste in a well at 8-10 Crosswall Street excavated in 1979, which was clearly derived from a late seventeenth-century bottle works (*74*), although its precise location has yet to be pin-pointed.

The one exception is the bottle furnace at Vauxhall Bridgefoot, on the opposite side of the road to the Duke of Buckingham's plate glasshouse. The earliest indication of glassmaking on the site comes from Thomas Hill's 1681 map of the Manor of Vauxhall. On the map it was annotated 'Mr Baker 4 tenements and the glasshouse'. John Baker inherited the plot in 1663, when no mention of the glasshouse is made, and it therefore must have been built sometime between then and the date of the map. Importantly, one tenant was listed as John Bellingham, the same man who had between 1671 and 1674 managed the nearby plate-glass works of Buckingham. It is therefore likely he actually built the furnace sometime after he left Buckingham's works in April 1674. In January 1685 Bellingham was awarded a letters patent to manufacture square-window glass for coaches and sash windows, although there is no direct evidence that these activities took

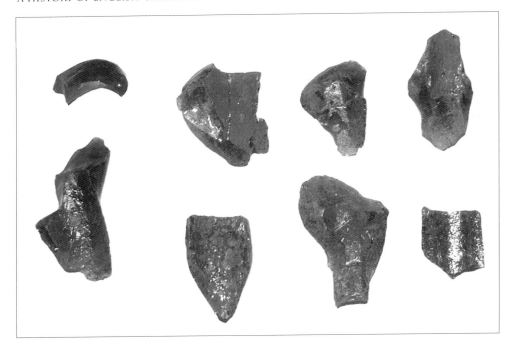

74 Moils from the production of wine bottles, found at Crosswall Street, London. *Author*

place at Vauxhall Bridgefoot. He seems to have continued to operate there until his death in 1700, when the works apparently ceased operation. Certainly by 1704 the remaining buildings on the plot were described as 'very old and ruinous'.

Excavations by the Museum of London Archaeology Service in 1989 revealed evidence for glassmaking in the area shown on Hill's 1681 map, although it is entirely probable that not all of the complex was exposed. Two distinct phases of glassmaking were revealed. The first was an unusual structure, which had subsequently been demolished, making its form hard to interpret (*75*). It was a brick-built rectangular structure 2.2m x 3.8m. On each of the two longer sides was a small rectangular D-shaped oven built through the wall, and in the centre of the structure were the remains of five pier bases, suggesting that it had a raised floor. This feature has been tentatively interpreted as a fritting oven; the two small side ovens would have produced heat that could have circulated evenly below the floor above, on which the raw ingredients could be heated to produce frit, but without fully fusing. The presence of unused lumps of frit in the last glassmaking phase of the site also supported this hypothesis.

The first-phase fritting oven was then demolished and cut through at its northern end by a larger melting furnace (*75*). Like Haughton Green, this was not of the familiar wing design, instead being a rectangular structure. The central furnace was brick-built and measured approximately 3m x 4m. The sieges were badly truncated by later levelling, but enough survived to suggest that it could have held three crucibles on each siege. As with Haughton Green and Kimmeridge, the flue at Vauxhall was deep and brick-lined for easy cleaning. At the western end there were the remains of stains that indicated that there once had been a set of doors to control the air flow, and the eastern end of the flue dog-legged to the south, presumably to fit in with a pre-existing boundary. The

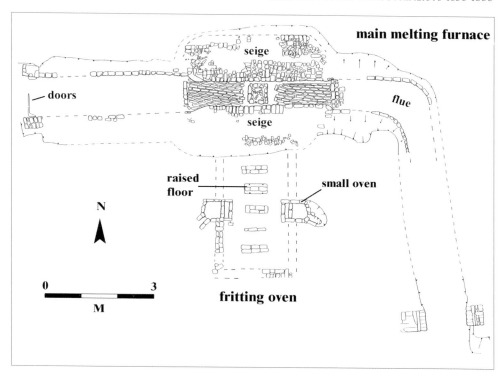

75 Plan of the furnace at Vauxhall Bridgefoot, London. *After Tyler and Willmott*

one new innovation in this design was that, instead of having fire bars on which the coal would have been placed suspended above the flue, there was actually a central pillar (*colour plate 22*).

Despite the fact that it is known that Bellingham was a specialist in plate-glass manufacture, there is no evidence that he practiced its production at the Vauxhall Bridgefoot furnace. The few pieces of unfinished plate glass found during the excavation are of a different chemical composition to the other glass from the site and probably came from Buckingham's furnace across the road. The majority of the glassworking waste consisted of green glass and, in the absence of evidence for ordinary window manufacture, bottles seem like the most likely product. Furthermore, fragments of half-finished and finished but unused bottles were common across the site. Most interesting of all was that, in the backfill of the main furnaces, dumped as part of the deliberate backfilling was a large quantity of crystalline material, which on chemical analysis proved to be frit of the same composition as the green bottle glass (*colour plate 23*). It is interesting to compare this material with experimental frit recreated in the laboratory (*colour plate 1*), and this is the first time frit has been positively recognised on any London site. Present in much smaller quantities was a clearer better-quality glass, both in the form of working waste and as half-finished vessels. Although clearly not of the same quality as the glass known to have been made by Ravenscroft and not lead-based, it would appear that Bellingham was also trying to make better-quality tablewares as well (*76*).

The Vauxhall Bridgefoot furnace is therefore a rare survivor for the period 1650-1700 in London, as it is the only site where both significant archaeological remains

76 Goblet made at Vauxhall Bridgefoot. *Author*

and historical documentation co-exists. Indeed it is unfortunate that, with the possible exception of Hopton Street, there is no comprehensive archaeological evidence for eighteenth-century glass production in the capital, despite the historical documentation. However, London was not the only place where production was flourishing at this time; other areas of the country were experiencing expansion and growth.

LATER PRODUCTION ELSEWHERE IN ENGLAND

While it is clear that, between the 1660s and the 1690s, there was a significant revival in glassmaking in London, the picture is less clear for these decades elsewhere in England. Glass was definitely being made in certain regional centres, such as Newcastle, although the scope and extent of this production is hard to quantify. Indeed, it is not until the last years of the seventeenth century that there is any indication of the wider national levels of production. The key document that changes this occurs in the letters of John Houghton, produced on the topic of the improvement of commerce and trade. In one particular letter dated 15 May 1696 he lists eighty-eight different furnaces that were in operation, and noted the nature of their production (*77*).

Location	County	Sorts of glass each house makes
In and around London and Southwark	–	9 for bottles, 2 for looking glass plates, 4 for crown glass and plates, 9 for flint and ordinary
Woolwich	Kent	1 for crown glass and plates, 1 flint glass and ordinary
Isle of Wight	Hampshire	1 flint glass and ordinary
Topsham nr Exon	Devonshire	1 for bottles
Odd Down nr Bath	Somersetshire	1 for bottles
Chellwood	Somersetshire	1 for window glass
In and about Bristol	–	5 for bottles, 1 for bottles and ordinary, 3 for flint glass and ordinary
Gloucester	Gloucestershire	3 for bottles
Newnham	Gloucestershire	2 bottle houses
Swansea	Glamorgan	1 for bottles
Oaken Gate	Shropshire	1 for bottles and window glass
Worcester	Worcestershire	1 for flint, green and ordinary
Coventry	Warwickshire	1 for flint, green and ordinary
Stourbridge	Worcestershire	7 for window glass, 5 for bottles, 5 for flint, green and ordinary
Near Liverpool	Lancashire	1 for flint, green and ordinary
Warrington	Lancashire	1 for window glass
Nottingham	Nottinghamshire	1 for bottles
Awsworth	Nottinghamshire	1 for flint, green and ordinary
Custom More	Nottinghamshire	1 for bottles
Nr Awsworth	Nottinghamshire	1 for flint, green and ordinary
Nr Silkstone	Yorkshire	1 for bottles
Nr Ferrybridge	Yorkshire	1 for bottles, 1 for flint, green and ordinary
King's Lynn	–	1 for bottles, 1 for flint, green and ordinary
Yarmouth	–	1 for bottles
Newcastle-upon-Tyne	Northumberland	6 for window glass, 4 for bottles, 1 for flint, green and ordinary

77 John Houghton's list of glass furnaces in England, 1696. *Adapted from Hartshorne*

This description is sometimes erroneously taken to be a comprehensive record of the whole industry, and there have been several attempts to link archaeological sites with those described by Houghton. While in some cases this can be successfully done, this approach assumes that Houghton knew of all furnaces in operation, which is unlikely given the dispersed nature of the industry. However, this list is useful in that it shows where the general concentrations of glassmaking were in the 1690s. Not unsurprisingly, London and Southwark were listed as having the greatest number of furnaces, with twenty-four in total, and these are described as being not only for the production of bottles and flint glass but also crown glass and mirror plates. The next highest concentration was the Stourbridge region, where seventeen glasshouses were listed, again for the production of window glass, bottles and vessels in roughly equal proportions. Close behind Stourbridge came Newcastle with eleven furnaces in total, but it is interesting to note that in this case the majority were for window glass production and only one was listed as being for vessels. The final concentration was at Bristol, where nine glasshouses were listed. Again, the proportion of types of glass made is interesting, as here production apparently concentrated on bottle and vessel glass, and windows are not mentioned.

While other areas were noted to have glasshouses, there were no other concentrated centres of production. Perhaps slight exceptions are Gloucestershire, where five furnaces were listed, and Nottinghamshire, where there were apparently four. However, while Houghton's list is inevitably a valuable assessment of the general state of the industry, there are archaeological sources that help provide a different and more comprehensive picture of the industry. A case in point is Yorkshire where, according to Houghton, only three furnaces were operating, suggesting that it was not of particular regional importance. However, this contrasts with the level of information gathered through historical and archaeological research.

Production in South Yorkshire

While it is recognised that Francis Bristow was briefly producing window glass under licence for Mansell at Wentworth near Rotherham between 1632–1642, the glass industry proper did not come established in the region until the mid-seventeenth century. At sometime around the year 1653 three members of the Pilmay family, John, Peter and Mary, moved from Haughton Green to Silkstone, near Barnsley, where they rented the mill from a local yeoman, William Scott, and set up a furnace. Shortly after, in 1655, Scott died and three years later on 26 September John Pilmay married his widow Abigail. The Pilmay's continued to make glass on the site and in 1675, when John died, the works were jointly taken over by Peter Pilmay and John's widow Abigail. During this period a number of glassmakers are known to have been working for the Pilmay's, and parish records record the names of John Townend, Ephraim Burdett and Francis Morton. Indeed, the works seem to have been of sufficient size to attract the interest of the antiquary Ralph Thoresby, who noted in his journal in 1682 that he 'went to Silkstone... and saw the glasshouse'.

In 1697 Peter Pilmay died childless, and the following year Abigail also died, leaving the works to John Scott, her eldest son from her first marriage. Interestingly, on Abigail's death a probate was drawn up that still survives. This listed that there were in fact two furnaces: the 'greenhouse' and the 'whitehouse', as well as 'tools belonging to bothe houses'. It therefore appears that, in 1698 at least, there were two types of production: green glass and white or quality clear glass. Furthermore, not only were the furnaces themselves described but also other goods and ingredients. These included rape ash,

Breeley sand, red lead and a 'blew powder', as well as moulds and clay for making crucibles. This picture is further confirmed by another inventory that survives for 1707, which stated that the green glasshouse had been shut down, but the other was still producing flint glass.

When the Silkstone works finally ceased operating is uncertain. But what is clear is that, despite being left it in her will, Abigail's son John Scott never actually ran the works. On Abigail's death it appears to have been effectively taken over by Francis Morton, who married Scott's daughter. Morton seems to have kept production going until 16 March 1732 when he himself died. It seems likely that the works then shut at this point, and certainly by 1758 a mortgage refers to 'land adjacent to the old glasshouse'.

Of the works themselves only a small amount is known archaeologically. Denis Ashurst identified the general location to be in the vicinity of a later eighteenth-century barn, which has subsequently been demolished. This general location has been confirmed recently by several small-scale excavations (78). Unfortunately no in situ remains of the furnace have been located, although crucibles, waste and glass fragments have been recovered. These are useful in confirming in part the documentary sources and show that a range of green glass, such as phials and wine bottles, was made at the site. Better-quality lead glass forms such as goblets and jellies, as well as coloured glasses decorated with opaque white flecks, were also identifiable in the excavated assemblage (*colour plate 24*).

Another site of similar date about which more is known is Bolsterstone, less than five miles to the south of Silkstone. As far as can be ascertained this site, unlike Silkstone, was not founded by immigrant glassmakers, although the documentation is far from complete in this regard. The first indication came from the records of the Fox family of Fulwood Hall, when it was noted that, sometime before his death in 1659, John Fox was making glass at Smithfield near Bradfield, but these works were short-lived and moved to Bolsterstone. On the death of John Fox his son George took over running the operation

78 Location of the furnace at Silkstone under excavation. *Author*

until he too died in 1692. In 1702 George's widow Mary married a Robert Blackburn, who may well have already been working under George, and he continued to manage the works. Glassmaking apparently flourished and another glassmaker, Richard Dixon, employed. At some point very early in the eighteenth century a William Fenney was also working there, and in 1718 he married the daughter of the late George and Mary Fox, also called Mary. Robert Blackburn remained in control until 1727 when he died and shortly after it appears there was a dispute between Fenney and his mother-in-law. The cause of this seems to have been Fenney's intention to build a second furnace in the near vicinity, much against Mary's wishes. This dispute was serious enough to prompt Mary to change her will in 1738, leaving the glasshouse to Michael Fox, her grandson from her first marriage, and the sum of £200 to each of Fenney's children. However, her generosity to Fenney's heirs had a proviso, which she noted to her executors:

> my son in law Willaim Fene las given mee such aprehencion of being troublesum by his design
> of setting up a Glashous at boulster stone made me alter my will… if he will give my executors
> such securitys as the approve that hee will not set up or ioyn whining ten miles of this place the
> pore children shall have there legacys.

The precise date of Mary's death is not known, but her wish that Fenney should not have any new connection with glassmaking within ten miles of Bolsterstone was respected. The furnace certainly continued production until at least 1758 when Michael Fox died, at which time it probably shut down and converted into a pottery kiln.

Although the precise location of the furnace remained unknown until nearly forty years ago, antiquarian sources had indicated the rough location, and the frequent finds of glass and crucible by residents around Pothouse Lane confirmed this. It was only when the site was threatened by road widening in 1968 that Denis Ashurst sought to precisely locate and excavate the furnace. It quickly became apparent that the building that housed the furnace was still standing largely intact, and that the subsurface features were very well preserved. Indeed, the archaeological remains uncovered by Ashurst were probably the most complex thus far found on an English glasshouse site.

The building in which the furnace was housed was rectangular with large arched openings on both sides, which led into now-demolished lead-to extensions (*colour figure 25*). Although the furnace structure had been largely removed later on, remaining below ground were two parallel siege benches roughly 2m long and flanking a main north-west-south-east running flue (*79*). This was well-built and stone-lined; however, there was also a secondary smaller flue running at right angles to this one providing a more complex system of air circulation. In the north-west wall of the building were the remains of two hearth openings, which Ashurst interpreted as the annealing ovens, although other interpretations are possible.

Also significant were the artefacts found by Ashurst during his excavation as well as in subsequent investigations. Most interesting of these were the remains of the crucibles, four of which have been left fused in situ on the siege benches when the furnace went out of use and was demolished. These were around 75cm in diameter and of a similar height. Two examples were 'open' and bucket-shaped, but two were a completely different type, being closed at the top, with access gained through a narrow opening (*80*). The glass in the open crucibles was a grey colour and quite gritty, while the glass from the closed crucibles was of a much better quality and colourless. This led Ashurst to suggest that the closed crucibles were used for a better-quality glass, as a way of avoiding contamination of the batch from fumes and ash within the furnace.

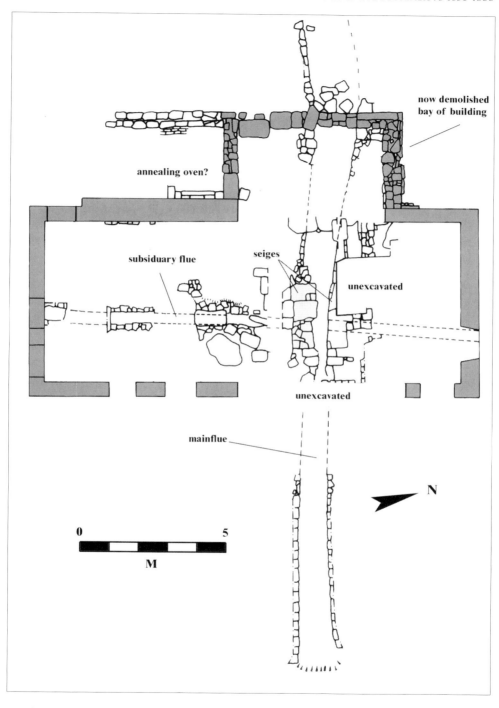

79 Plan of the glass furnace at Bolsterstone. *After Ashurst*

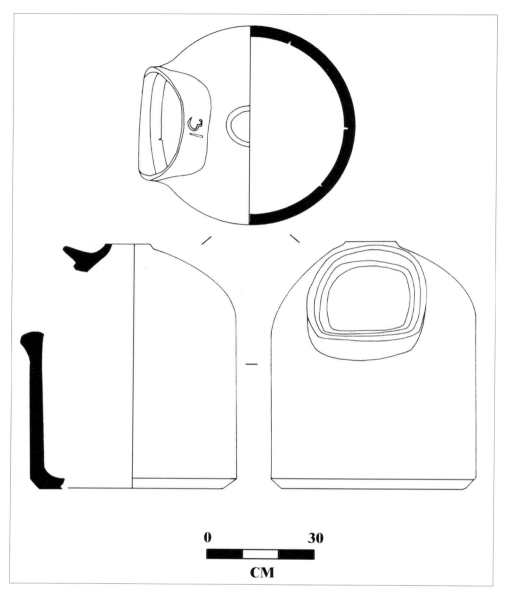

80 Closed crucible from Bolsterstone. *After Ashurst*

The glass finds were also very revealing. These included the remains of clear window glass, but also, much more unusually, very fine cobalt blue and purple window crowns (*colour plate 26*). This interestingly confirms an inventory of Robert Blackburn's stock, undertaken on 16 August 1727, which included a large number of window panes. Another product that was clearly a staple of the furnace was the wine bottle, which could be identified from numerous fragments, but also from the finding of two pipe-clay stamps used to impress the glass seal on the bottle when it was still molten. Unfortunately these are now lost, but one was decorated with an animal head motif and the other a letter 'G'. Also made in a green glass were phials and other small bottles, while fragments of half-made lead glass goblets, beakers and jugs were also found. The final types of vessel encountered were those made in coloured glasses of primarily black, blue, amber and purple, although these were usually too fragmented for positive identification of their precise form. However, what was most significant, and similar to those found at Silkstone, was that many of these were decorated with small flecks (or in occasional examples trailed loops) of opaque white glass that had been smoothed into the surface (*colour plate 26*). The finding of this type of glass at both Silkstone and Bolsterstone is particularly significant, as it is a decorative scheme normally thought to have been first produced at Nailsea, Bristol, but during the early nineteenth century. Its occurrence on two Yorkshire sites over 100 years earlier must represent a hitherto unrecognised regional tradition.

The changing of her will by Mary Fox in 1738 seems to have made William Fenney reconsider his ambitions to construct another furnace, and he was forced to look elsewhere. Two years later in 1740 he founded a new works at Catcliffe, just over eleven miles as the crow flies from Bolsterstone. The reason for his eagerness to build a new furnace despite the fact the old one at Bolsterstone was clearly still successful, can be seen in his choice of design at Catcliffe. At once he set about building two furnaces of radically different, and still relatively innovative, form. These had the usual melting furnace, but one that was enclosed in a large open-topped cone structure, which had the effect of massively increasing the amount of draft drawn through the furnace.

Fenney's cones at Catcliffe were by no means the earliest built. The origin of the design is obscure, but it is possible the technological idea was transferred from the bottle kiln that was increasingly used in ceramic production. However, it is known that, by 1694, cones were built at Gloucester and Topsham in Devon, and as early as 1696 Captain Philip Roche had built one at Dublin. Where Fenney drew his inspiration from is unclear, but it clearly represented a considerable financial investment for him. Two cones were built and one still stands, making it the earliest surviving anywhere in the country (*colour plate 27*). This currently stands 18.5m, 1.5m of which is constructed of sandstone and the rest of brick. The structure is pierced with a number of doors and openings, although it is clear that some of these were added later on in its life.

In 1962, in advance of threatened demolition, Geoffrey Lewis from Sheffield Museums undertook a partial clearance of the site, although this was hastily recorded and never properly published. The only records surviving are a sketch plan (*81*) and some contemporary photographs. This plan shows that externally at least one building adjoined the cone, and others can be seen in the ephemeral remains of rooflines visible in some original excavation photographs, but these have been long since removed by more modern repointing (*82*). Internally the central furnace was destroyed, but Lewis's excavation revealed the remains of a single large flue to channel air into the central furnace (*83*).

Despite his optimism in building two cones, Fenney appears to have had little financial success in his venture and, in 1759, was forced to sell up to the May family. The works continued in operation under a variety of ownerships until 1884 when it closed, briefly reopening for less than a year in 1901. Lewis's excavation revealed virtually nothing of the products of the early phase of the furnace, but it is not unreasonable to suppose they included both bottles and drinking glasses.

The last South Yorkshire site of this period for which there is surviving archaeological evidence is at Gawber, which lies two miles north-east of Barnsley. The origins and first phase of this site are unknown historically. However, by the 1730s, a William Thorpe

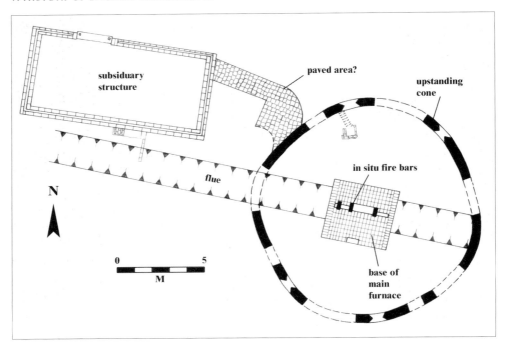

Above: *81* Plan of the excavated furnace at Catcliffe. *After Lewis*

Left: *82* Roof lines visible on the cone at Catcliffe. *G. Lewis*

83 Excavation in the interior of the cone at Catcliffe. *G. Lewis*

took out a lease on Gawber Hall and at the same time the parish registers record an influx of glassmakers, the first being 'Henry son of William Morton glassmaker born 7 January'. These references continue in the registers until 1818 and, in total, twenty-two different families associated with the industry can be identified. Throughout this period the Thorpe family are listed as leasing the works, until finally, in the early nineteenth century, Samuel Thorpe decided to concentrate his efforts on exploiting the Barnsley Coalfield. In 1821 the works was sold and the furnace dismantled.

In 1964 Denis Ashurst started the attempt to locate the Thorpe works, and trial trenching initially located workshop buildings and a store, as well as associated dumps of waste, but not a furnace. However, over the next three years and immediately to the north of this area, Ashurst was able to locate and excavate the furnace, which had two distinct, and very different, phases.

The first was a small structure, heavily truncated by later activity on the site. What was evident, though, was a small rectangular furnace about 3m long and 2m wide. The only element that survived to any degree was the central flue, which was flagged, and some crucible fragments that showed that a clear glass was being produced. Interestingly, an archaeomagnetic date of the siege bench revealed that the last firing of the structure came between 1690-1735, presumably just prior to Thorpe's acquisition of the site. Further to this, little else concerning its form or products could be ascertained.

The second phase was built almost directly over the first furnace and, being considerably more substantial, must relate to Thorpe's tenure of the site. Again no superstructure survived, but Ashurst's excavation revealed over three-quarters of the ground plan (*84*). At the centre lay the actual melting furnace, but unfortunately it was so truncated by subsequent demolition most of its internal features could not be seen. This was originally

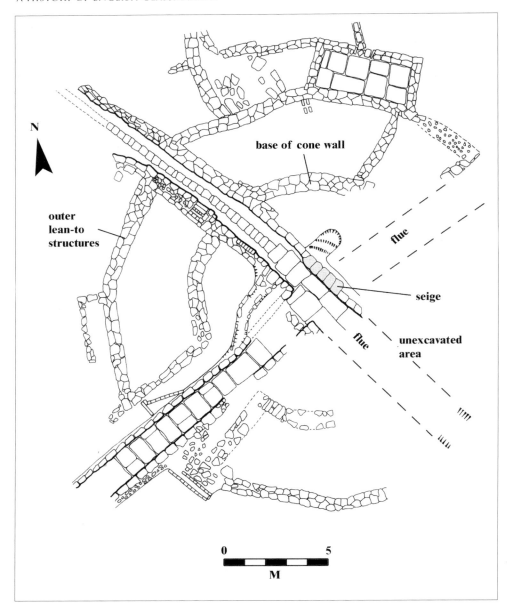

84 Plan of the cone at Gawber. *After Ashurst*

fed by a single north–south running flue around 1m–1.5m wide. However, at a later date a second flue running east–west and at right angles to the first was inserted to increase the provision of air, although when this modification took place is unclear.

Surrounding the central furnace structure was a circular stone foundation between 12m–13m in diameter, and this was the very lowest course of a large cone structure. Outside of this was a second sub-circular foundation 20m–21m in diameter and divided into sections or compartments. This outer foundation was originally thought erroneously to be the actual wall of the cone, but it is now clear that this was a series of lean-to buildings attached to the outer wall of the cone, similar to Catcliffe.

As well as the structural remains of the glasshouse, Ashurst recovered many associated finds. There were numerous pieces of crucible, often too fragmented to reconstruct but, where this was possible, they were always of the open-bucket shape, and not closed as at Bolsterstone. A large quantity of waste glass was also found and the majority of this was green or brown, although some clear and even blue glass was recovered. Products that could be identified included a large quantity of wine bottles and phials, and these were probably the main output of the furnace. Indeed, what was distinctive were the numbers of different wine bottle seals found. Finewares produced included goblets, cups and jellies; again forms typical of the eighteenth century.

Production in and Around Stourbridge

In 1696 Houghton listed seventeen glasshouses in operation in and around Stourbridge: seven for windows, five for bottles and five for vessels. Whether this is the exact number in operation at the time is uncertain, but it does reflect the genuine importance of Stourbridge in the national picture during the late seventeenth century, and one that continued for over 200 years. Considerable historical information for individual glassworks survives; indeed a recent survey of the industry by Jason Ellis has identified forty-nine different works in the Stourbridge and Dudley region dating to between the seventeenth and twentieth centuries. While it is not the purpose to reiterate all these here, an examination of some of the historical background to the industry, and recent archaeological investigations in particular, is important.

The earliest reference to glassmaking in the area came between 1610-1614, when Paul Tyzack founded the Coleman's glasshouse at Lye just one mile to the east of Stourbridge town centre. He worked under licence from Mansell and produced window glass. This works continued under management of the Tyzack family until 1658 when it was destroyed by a fire. The furnace was rebuilt but a series of disputes with the landowner, John Lyddiat, ensued, which eventually led to ejection of the Tyzacks, and the works appear to have ceased operation.

Another early establishment was the Ridgrave glasshouse. This was established at Hungary Hill, also just to the east of Stourbridge, by members of the Henzey family and the suggestion is that this took place sometime between 1612-1630. However, the first proper documentation did not occur until 1699 when it was owned by a John Wheeler. On his death in 1708 Wheeler bequeathed it to his son, also called John, who continued operations, although it was eventually taken over by a John Hill until its closure in the 1770s. Other furnaces in the region also had origins in the first half of the seventeenth century, such as the Holloway glasshouse at Amblecote, established in 1623, and the Heath glassworks in Stourbridge founded in 1636.

However, there are several sites worth mentioning in slightly more detail partly because they are good examples of documented works, but also because they have received more recent, if unpublished, archaeological investigation. Among these are the Dial glasshouses. The first of these furnaces was built in 1704 by Thomas Henzey, who secured a ninety-nine-year lease on Brettell Lane to produce cylinder window glass. Thomas died in 1712 leaving the furnace to his three sons, who continued to work there until 1738, when the last of them died without issue. With the cessation of Henzey involvement, the site was initially taken over by John Pidcock and John Goodwin although, in 1747, Pidcock took sole control. Pidcock was clearly successful in his running of the works, as demonstrated by an advertisement that appeared in 1761 declaring:

> Wanted in the broad glass and bottle glass trade, several hands, viz. workmen, blowers, gatherers, founders and teezers. any such by applying to Mr Pidcock at the Dial Glasshouse near Stourbridge, will meet with great encouragement and constant employment.

The works continued making window glass until 1788 when, due to the cutting of a new canal, John Pidcock decided to relocate the furnace. Unfortunately, archaeologically little is known of the first furnace although when unmonitored redevelopment of the site took place in 1992 quantities of glass and crucible were apparently observed.

Pidcock's relocation of the Dial furnace placed the new site right on the bank of the canal. It is known that he built two new cones but shortly after, in 1791, he died. His surviving will indicates that he had become a wealthy man from his commercial activities, so it is not surprising that the furnace continued to be worked under a variety of subsequent owners and managers until finally it was bought in 1922 by Plowden & Thompson, who still own the site today. Of the two later cones, rather more is known about the first Dial works. In 1866, shortly before its conversion into an iron foundry, one of the cones was surveyed (85). This shows it to have been around 18.5m in diameter with two intersecting flues and a series of attached outbuildings. The second cone survived rather longer until 1935, when it was truncated and the insides cleared. This cone is in existence today and still retains the foundation datestone of 1788 (colour plate 28).

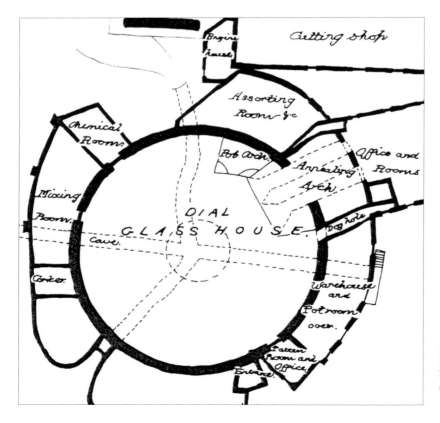

85 New Dial cone, Stourbridge survey of 1866

Two other sites with less certain origins are worthy of brief mention. The first was the Canalside Glassworks at Audnam. Founded for the purpose of producing bottles sometime between 1788 and 1816 by the Grazebrook family, this too was positioned by the newly built canal. The site was in operation until 1883, when it was converted into an iron and brass foundry. Recent excavations by the Historic Environment Team of Dudley Metropolitan Borough Council revealed a demolished cone 19m in diameter at its base (86). Interestingly the central furnace, which was completely destroyed, was originally fed by a long central flue, met at an angle by a second flue on the western side, although this did not bisect it as at Gawber or the New Dial cone. A further site of interest was at Redhouse Lane, Wordsley. This was originally sold on 21 June 1788 to Richard Bradley, in partnership with George Ensell, who started to produce cylinder window glass. Constructed on the site was a cone 90ft tall and 60ft in diameter (87), and the site continued to produce glass until 1936. The cone still survives intact today and is a museum. Furthermore, it still maintains the only surviving example of an innovative type of mechanised annealing oven developed by Ensell.

Production in and Around Bristol

Bristol was another area where glassmaking was taking place within a concentrated area. Houghton indicated that by 1696 there were at least nine furnaces working here. However, the earliest reference to the industry at Bristol comes in 1651 when it was noted that there was 'an ingenious glass-maker Master Edward Dagney, an Italian then living in

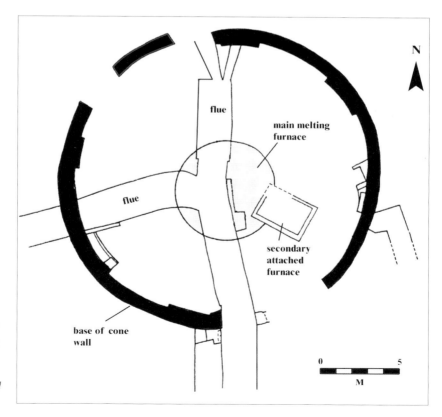

86 Plan of the cone at Canalside, Audnam. *After Boland and Ellis*

flue

main melting furnace

flue

secondary attached furnace

base of cone wall

N

0   5
M

87 The Redhouse cone, taken in 1909

Bristow'. Little more is known of this man, although his sons were to feature prominently in the Newcastle industry, and it is not until the 1670s, when eleven separate applications were made by glassmakers for admission to the freedom of the city, that glassmaking can be said to have become firmly established. Of the nine furnaces listed by Houghton, it is interesting that over half were for the production of bottles, and this might suggest a connection between the output and the developing transatlantic trade that demanded a large number of containers. It is also interesting to note that English wine bottles are common finds, often in huge numbers, on early colonial sites such as Jamestown and Williamsburg. It is entirely probable that many were made in the Bristol area.

One of the earliest of these operations was at Redcliff Backs. Although the precise date for its foundation is unknown, it was certainly working by the end of the seventeenth century. Owned by Lowden family, one of whom had petitioned for admission to the freedom of the city in 1673, the works was intended for the production of quality vessel glass. The site changed hands a number of times during the eighteenth century, once going bankrupt in 1760 when it was described as making 'the best white and flint wares'. Production was revived until 1802 when it closed down for the final time.

Another early furnace is known in the near vicinity at St Thomas Street and this was owned by Richard Warren. An indication of the range of products made at the furnace can be seen in an advertisement on 17 May 1712 in *The Post Man*, which stated that:

> At Mr Richard Warrens and Company's Glasshouse in St Thomas Street, Bristol are to be sold all sorts of very good Crown Glass, wholesale or retale; and at the same house are made all sorts of very good Bottles; all sold cheape as at any place in England.

In 1773, six years after Warren's death, the cone collapsed during a storm so suddenly that it 'occasioned such a shock that the neighbours, who were in their beds, were greatly alarmed apprehending it to be an earthquake'. It was quickly rebuilt and the St Thomas Street works continued in operation until 1802.

With the broadening of the river Avon in the 1710s and 1720s, new glasshouses emerged in this area. One of the best documented was at Cheese Lane by the later St Philip's Bridge. It was probably founded around 1710, although the first record appeared with the announcement of another disaster, this time reported in the *General Advertiser* on 8 June 1736:

> On Friday last about 11 o'clock in the forenoon a large glasshouse belonging to Sir Abraham Elton Bart near the Ferry in St Philips, suddenly fell down; happy it was for the glass-men that the fire was out, and only some few masons were employed in the repair of it. We hear but of one man who received any hurt, and that not dangerous.

The Eltons were a mercantile family and not glassmakers themselves, and who managed the operation initially is not known. Sir Abraham's son, also called Abraham, took on apprentices until he died in 1741, and the works were then managed by Daniel Taylor, but still controlled by the Elton family. Abraham's will mentions the works as producing crown glass and this seems to have been the staple product until 1809, when the furnace closed and the cone became a warehouse until its eventual demolition. An excavation in 2001 by the Bristol and Region Archaeological Services on the site revealed the remains of the furnace. Later features heavily truncated the archaeology, but a small amount of the cone wall was found, as well as associated buildings and the remains of glassworking waste and crucibles.

One furnace with a long history of production was the Hoopers' works on Avon Street. Built in 1720 by a large partnership of seventeen different people headed by Robert Hiscox, its primary products were wine bottles, which were exported to Portugal, France and the New World. In 1767 the works came up for sale and interestingly, as well as the buildings, a quantity of sand, clay and kelp were included in the auction. Being a going concern the works were bought up and run by a succession of owners until 1824, when it came under part-ownership of the Powells. For just under a century it continued to trade until it finally closed on 13 July 1923.

The only site in Bristol where there are any upstanding remains of a cone is on Prewitt Street. Here the lower portion of a truncated cone survives, cleared internally and now part of a hotel complex. Unfortunately virtually nothing is known of this glasshouse; no owners were recorded and its products cannot be identified. All that is known is that the site was taken over in 1812 and converted to the manufacture of chemicals.

In total at least sixteen different glasshouses were known to have been founded and been in operation within the limits of Bristol during the eighteenth century. An interesting source who visited Bristol at the height of the industry was Reinhold Angerstein. Angerstein was an official of the Swedish board of mines who toured Europe for six years, eighteen months of which was spent in England. He had a particular interest in industry and this was more than likely fuelled by the lucrative potential for industrial espionage. On 1 June 1754 he arrived in Bristol and observed that there were fifteen furnaces for the production of bottles alone, although not all were actually in operation. But what is important is that he gives the most comprehensive description of a glasshouse and in particular the melting furnace, which is fortunate as this is the portion that rarely survives to the present day:

> Inside, the furnace is built like any other glass furnace with calcinating furnaces on the side. The work is done with four crucibles or pots, two on each side, opposite each other. The other two sides that cross are the fireplaces, to throw in the coal that rests on thick two-inch-square iron bars. The furnace proper is vaulted underneath, like an adit, with two openings on the fireplaces, to provide draft for the furnaces and fireplaces. The high and the lower wall around the glass furnace only serves as a chimneystack to carry away the smoke. It is generally seventy to eighty feet high and made from brick masonry. The glass furnace proper is made of Stourbridge clay, two feet long five feet wide and six inches thick.

He also stated that, instead of sand, a mixture of Stourbridge clay and crushed brick was used for the manufacture of glass, as well as other ingredients that included sea sand, soap ash, 'shrope' (a bluish iron slag), Welsh kelp, limestone and old bottles.

Angerstein also mentions that there were five furnaces for the production of window glass, although not all of these were still active. This suggests that, by the mid-eighteenth century, there was already a possible decline in the fortunes of the Bristol industry. This can only have been made worse in 1775 by the enforced embargo placed on British goods by many of the North American colonies, shortly followed by the War of Independence. Coupled with the application of excise duties during the late eighteenth century, it is no surprise that the industry went into terminal decline so that, by 1835, when a commission examined the state of the industry, it reported that only five glasshouses were left working in Bristol.

The final site in the region that has its origin in the late eighteenth century was not established in Bristol itself but at Nailsea, eight miles to the west of the city. The works were associated with the Lucas family, the first member of which, Robert, came to Bristol from Worcestershire and set up a cider works. He clearly appreciated the advantage of investing in the glass industry, which may well have supplied containers for his cider, and he had shares in a furnace at Limekiln Lane in Bristol, which specialised in bottle production. When Robert died in 1774 his business interests passed to his son John. In addition to his existing stake in the Limekiln Lane works, John Lucas also took out a lease in 1787 on a pre-existing furnace at Stanton Wick to the south of Bristol. In the following year he leased unoccupied land at Nailsea Heath for the purpose of erecting a new furnace that was to trade under the name Nailsea Crown Glass & Glass Bottle Manufacturers. This new venture was not without setbacks: just two years after its founding the *Bristol Gazette* noted on 6 May 1790 that a 'fire at the new glass house… burnt off part of the roof… other parts of the buildings belonging to both crown glasshouses were preserved'. This is an intriguing reference, as it seems to suggest that there were at least two furnaces in operation at this stage.

Shortly after its foundation the works at both Nailsea and Stanton Wick were taken into a wider partnership between John Lucas, William Chance, Edward Homer and William Coathupe. It is intriguing to note that when this partnership was later renewed in 1807 it was stated that, of the £60,000 capital invested in the properties, Lucas held fifty-five per cent, Chance and Homer both fourteen per cent and Coathupe seventeen per cent, all considerable sums. An indication of the scale of the works at Nailsea can be gained from several sources. In 1792 it was noted that:

> A manufacture of crown plate glass has lately been established here (Nailsea) by Mr John Robert Lucas, of Bristol, at which a great number of hands are employed, and a range of houses, forming as it were a small colony, is erected for the habitation of the workmen and their families.

This is further confirmed by a plan of the works that still survives in the Bristol Record Office (*88*). Although drawn in the 1830s, it nevertheless confirms in part the description of 1791. At the heart of the works was Cone No. 1, the original furnace, and attached to this were pot rooms, a counting house and warehouses. Associated with this complex were rooms for breaking kelp, frit and a 'caulker' although the precise function of this room is unclear. Also in this area were two further furnaces marked Cone No. 2 and Cone No. 3, although these are nineteenth century in date. Further to the west was a large cone, No. 4 (not shown on *88*), and this appears to be very similar to the no. 1 furnace. However, excavations in the 1980s revealed that this was probably a slightly later furnace, known as the New House Cone, and built between 1826-9. What is particularly interesting is the long row of purpose-built housing to the north of the complex, consistent with the 1791 description of specific buildings erected for the habitation of the workers, and it is not hard to see why the site was described as a colony.

The Nailsea glassworks continued to grow through the nineteenth century. Although ownership changed during this time it continued to be successful, so much so that, in 1833, enough glass was being produced so that it paid over £33,000 in excise duty. However, changing economic fortunes, followed by a collapse of one of the principal cones in 1862, hastened its end and by May 1873 all production had ceased.

Production in and Around Newcastle

Newcastle was the last area where Houghton's list of 1696 suggested that there was a significant concentration of glassmaking. He recorded eleven furnaces in total, six for windows, four for bottles and just a single furnace for flint and ordinary glass. This reflects

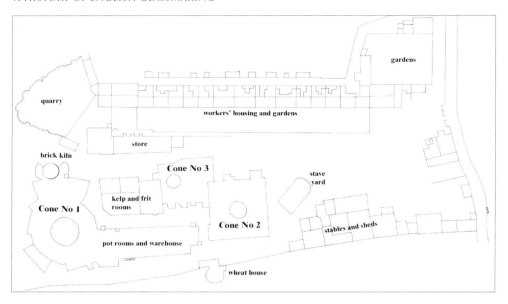

88 Plan of the Nailsea glassworks, 1830s

the pattern already started earlier in the century when, as already discussed, Mansell had successfully established a base for the production of window and bottle glass.

The single furnace identified by Houghton as producing vessel glass may well be that noted as being run by members of the Italian Dagnia family. The first member to be recorded in connection with the glass industry was Edward Dagney, working in 1651 in Bristol. However, in 1684, his three sons Onesiphorus, Edward and John, moved to Newcastle where they established a vessel glass furnace at Closegate.

In 1730 John Williams joined the Dagnias and married the widow of the recently deceased Onesiphorus. He seems to have rapidly taken over the running of the Closegate works, and the remaining Dagnia brothers relocated to South Shields, where little more was recorded of their glassmaking activities. Williams continued to run the works successfully until 1775 when it was bought out by Cookson and Airey, although it continued to operate well into the nineteenth century.

Other long-established glassworks were also changing hands at this time. In 1759 the furnace at Howden Pans, originally established by Mansell and subsequently run after his death by the Henzey family, was sold to Matthew Ridley. His son, also named Matthew, later gained control in 1765 of remaining works held by the Henzeys elsewhere in the town, making the Ridleys the predominant bottle producers in Newcastle. Williams and Ridley were just two of a number of individuals who were responsible for a flourishing industry in the region. This was not just restricted to the north bank of the Tyne; during the eighteenth century glassworks are known to have been operating in Gateshead and South Shields as well. Indeed, by 1769 John Hopton had established a glasshouse at Sunderland for the production of flint glass. Such was the strength of the regional industry that the *England Gazette* for 1751 was caused to note that 'the number of ships employed carrying not only coals and salt, but glass… to diverse parts of the kingdom as well as abroad makes it a fine nursery for seamen'.

Given this position of strength, it is perhaps unfortunate that very little is known of them archaeologically. This is in large part due to the subsequent redevelopment of both banks of the Tyne in the late nineteenth and twentieth centuries. Today, while dumps of glassworking waste are not uncommon finds, none can be related to specific works.

One exception to this is the glassworks at Lemington, which lies on the north bank of the Tyne less than five miles to the west of Newcastle city centre. The industry was established here in 1787, when the newly founded Northumberland Glass Company obtained the leasehold of the site from the Duke of Northumberland. A single cone was built with the intention to produce flint glass, and this appears on John Gibon's Tyne Colliery Plan of 1788. The site was rapidly developed, as in 1825 Eneas Mackenzie noted that 'within a short time there were three more (cones), including one very lofty and built of brick'. The site continued to produce flint glass until, in 1906 it was bought by the General Electric Company to produce light bulbs and tubing (*89*). Until its final closure in 1996, the works continued to develop and grow, but this caused the removal of many of the earlier buildings and features.

Luckily, despite this wholesale redevelopment of the site, the cone of 1787 survived demolition. It is circular in plan with a diameter of 23m and a surviving height of 39m, although it was probably originally a little taller (*90*). In its first phase the cone was pierced by eleven openings, some leading to now demolished lean-to structures, others just to allow the control of the draft. Unfortunately it is impossible to reconstruct the original eighteenth-century furnace or its associated features any further due to later disturbance. Nonetheless, the Lemington cone remains an impressive reminder of a feature that would have been a common sight to any travelling on the Tyne.

LEMINGTON GLASS WORKS OF THE GENERAL ELECTRIC C⁰ L꜒ᴰ
LEMINGTON ON TYNE

89 The Lemington works photographed in 1903

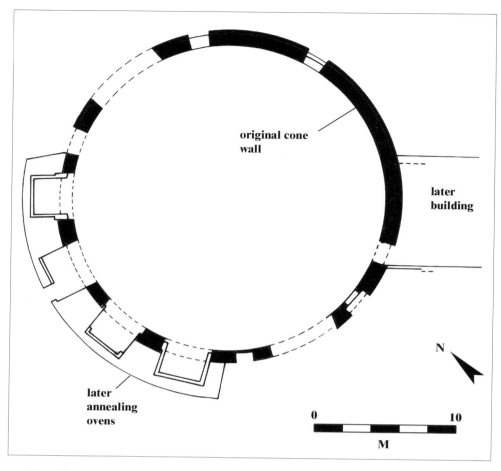

90 Plan of the Lemington Cone. *After RCHM*

POSTSCRIPT: THE NINETEENTH CENTURY

By the start of the nineteenth century the English glass industry was at an eve of a revolution. This did not happen overnight and for many working in the business a far gloomier future might have been anticipated. In many locations glass production was actually shrinking in the latter part of the eighteenth century and, although the figures quoted in contemporary historical sources are far from precise, they do give a general indication of the health of the industry. In London, for example, Houghton states there were twenty-four furnaces in 1696, while by 1755 Stow's Street Survey suggests that this had shrunk to fourteen. In 1833 a parliamentary inquiry observed that there were just three furnaces operating in the capital, and one of these was relatively new. Such a pattern was mirrored in other, but not all, locations around Britain; most notably at Bristol. While the number of furnaces operating was not necessarily indicative of the scale of manufacture, individual factories could have operated on a large scale and had far higher rates of production, it does suggest that the situation was changing.

One explanation for the decline in production was the passing of the Excise Act of 1745. This was not the first time glass production had been subject to taxation; between September 1695 and August 1699 there was an emergency tax placed on glass to help fund the French war, although this was bitterly opposed and finally withdrawn. Whereas this earlier tax had been levied against the value of the glasses, the new Excise Act taxed by weight. So successful was this that the rates were doubled in 1777, and further increases happened during the 1780s. To make the situation worse the English industry was facing greater competition from abroad, and most notably Ireland, where production in Dublin, Cork and Waterford in particular was becoming more firmly established.

The full effects of the excise duty on the industry became fully apparent in the first decades of the nineteenth century and, in 1833, a Royal Commission was formed to investigate the now-parlous condition of the industry, which it reported had nearly halved its output since the imposition of the tax. Given this, and after some delay, the Excise Act was finally repealed in 1845.

With these financial restraints removed, the industry was in a far better position to flourish during the second half of the nineteenth century. This it did indeed do, for several main reasons. With the Great Exhibition in 1851 there was a renewed interest in many crafts and industries, and glass was no exception. Indeed, the building of the Crystal Palace itself provided a massive boost to the firm of Chance Brothers in Birmingham, who were required to produced the 293,665 panes of glass to cover the 900,000 square feet that had to be glazed, at that point the largest ever commission of glass for a specific building project. But what also resulted was a renewed desire for glass and an appetite among the growing middle classes for fashionable and decorative items.

Traditional manufacturing processes could not meet this enhanced demand and, therefore, it is not surprising that new technologies developed rapidly. The first of these was the evolution of pressed glass, whereby molten glass could be mechanically forced into complex shapes. Although the first machines for this were developing in the 1820s, it was only by the time of the Great Exhibition that glassmakers were able to rapidly produce decorative tablewares at a fraction of the cost of more traditionally produced wares. Furthermore, the introduction of mechanised pressing created brand-new products and markets. The most successful of these businesses to develop was concerned with manufacturing containers. With the development of bottle-making machines, tailor-made containers could be mass-produced, and the second half of the nineteenth century saw glass become for the first time a truly disposable consumer item.

Hand-in-hand with these developments came other technological advances in the composition of glass and the design of furnaces. For example, from the 1860s onwards a new much-cheaper glass, using bicarbonate of soda rather than soda ash or lead, was developed first in the United States, but subsequently adopted elsewhere. Glassmakers had, throughout the eighteenth and early nineteenth centuries, been seeking innovative ways to build more efficient furnaces and, with the advent of the mass production of glass, those with far larger capacities were clearly needed. This culminated in the invention of the regenerative furnace by the Siemen brothers, first built in 1860 at Rotherham, and for which they subsequently were granted a patent in 1870. The regenerative furnace was completely novel in design; fired by gas, it recycled rather than released its hot exhaust glasses. This not only reduced fuel use; it resulted in far higher temperatures being achieved. Furthermore, it was possible for large 'tank' furnaces to be built, continuously fired and fed with raw materials, and through the clever use of a barrier only the perfectly melted batch was allowed to flow into a second chamber where it could be worked.

The consequence of both the increasing scales of production and the growing demand for glass by consumers during the nineteenth century was felt across the country. New factories appeared in many regions, although London never regained its former importance. For example, Ashurst documented the number of known works in the relatively small region of South Yorkshire. In 1800 there were just four recorded furnaces; by the turn of the next century there were at least twenty-five factories. The glass industry had reached its zenith.

GLOSSARY

Archaeomagnetic dating: The technique whereby samples taken from hearths or furnaces can be dated. Iron particles within the clay, when heated above a certain temperature, align with magnetic north. On comparison with the known historical location of magnetic north the sample can be given a date range for its last firing.

Annealing: The process whereby the finished glass vessel is slowly cooled in a controlled way to prevent the build-up of internal stresses that could lead to the shattering of the vessel.

Batch: The mixture formed in the crucible when silica, alkali and lime are fused in the furnace.

Blowing iron: A tubular metal pipe with a wooden holding end for the inflation of glass.

Came: An 'H'-shaped lead strip used to hold individual flat quarries to form a window pane.

Cane: A collection of thin glass rods that are fused together to produce a mono or polychrome rod for surface decoration of glass vessels.

Cristallo: A form of high-quality soda glass, first developed in Venice during the fifteenth century using barilla as a flux.

Crizzling: A glass disease that affected early lead crystal and some forms of soda glass. The lack of lime in the batch caused small stress cracks to form in the vessel, which often lead to its crumbling and disintegration.

Crown glass: A type of window glass formed by opening out and spinning a large paraison of glass into a circular sheet. This is then cut into individual quarries.

Crucible: The ceramic container in which the batch is melted in the furnace.

Cylinder glass: A type of window glass made by the blowing and opening out of a large tube of glass. This produced a larger area of glass sheet than crown glass.

Cullet: Scrap glass from old vessels collected by the glassmaker for recycling. Cullet also served to lower the melting temperature of the batch.

***Façon de Venise*:** The traditional term used to describe the high-quality soda or mixed alkali glass made in Northern Europe, thought to be in imitation of Venetian styles.

Flue: The air channel, which is often underground, which feeds air into the furnace.

Forest Glass: A type of glass traditionally made in wooded areas, which uses potash derived from burnt wood as its alkali. Green in colour, it weathers easily in archaeological contexts.

Free blowing: The principle technique of fashioning a vessel by inflating a gather of glass on the end of a blowing iron.

Frit: A semi-fused compound of the glass ingredients formed by a solid-state reaction at around 700°C. Frit is not a fully vitrified material, but appears as a granular substance, which is subsequently ground and melted into a fully formed glass.

Gather: The portion of molten glass on the end of the blowing iron, which is subsequently inflated to form the vessel.

Gathering hole: The orifice through which the blowing iron is inserted to take a gather of glass. Sometimes known colloquially as the 'glory hole'.

Jacks: A pair of sprung pincers used by the glassmaker to constrict or open out the paraison being shaped.

Lead crystal: A type of glass developed in the 1670s using up to thirty per cent lead oxide. Traditionally its development has been accredited to Ravenscroft, and the medium soon became the dominant metal for finewares of the eighteenth century.

Lehr: An alternative glassworking name for an annealing oven.

Marver: The process of rolling the paraison on a flat block, usually made of marble, to either shape the vessel or impress applied cane decoration.

Merese: A disk of glass applied between the bowl or the foot and the stem of a goblet to provide a decorative join.

Metal: A sometimes ambiguous term, but used here to refer to the consistency of the glass, much in the same way as the term 'fabric' is used in a pottery description. Usually used to differentiate between potash and soda glasses.

Moil: The circular ring of glass that remains on the blowing iron once the vessel being formed is removed.

Mould blowing: The inflation of a paraison into a fixed two-piece mould. The glass is pressed against the side of the mould assuming its shape and is only removed when it is cool enough to hold its new form.

Over-blow: An excess portion of glass from the paraison that is cracked off and discarded when certain vessel types are being manufactured.

Paraison: The gather on the end of the blowing iron that is already slightly inflated.

Pontil iron: A metal rod that is applied to the base of a vessel with a blob of glass during manufacture, usually so it can be held to form the rim. When removed it leaves a slight scar on the glass.

Potash glass: A green-tinted glass made with a potash alkali, often manufactured in woodland areas (see forest glass), but also produced in urban locations.

Prunt: Decoration consisting of an applied blob of glass. These can be further manipulated by pulling or, in the case of roemers, stamping.

Quarry: A small shaped pane of window glass, cut from either a crown or a cylinder and held together with lead cames.

Siege: The bench inside the furnace on which the crucibles sit.

Soda glass: A type of glass traditionally associated with the more specialised glassworks that used soda as its alkali.

FURTHER READING

I INTRODUCTION: THE NATURE AND FORMATION OF GLASS

Charleston, R. (1978) 'Glass furnaces through the ages', *Journal of Glass Studies* **20**, 9-33

Gudenrath, W. (1991) 'Techniques of glassmaking and decoration', in Tait, H (ed.) *Five Thousand Years of Glass*. British Museum Press, 213-241

Newton, R. & Davidson, S. (1989) *Conservation of Glass*. Butterworths

2 ROMAN BEGINNINGS AD 43-500

Allen, D. (1998) *Roman Glass in Britain*, Shire Books

Follman-Schulz, A. (1991) 'Fours de verriers romains dans la province de Germainie Inférieure', in D. Foy & Sennequier *Ateliers de Verriers de l'Antiquité à la période Pré-instrielle*. Rouen, l'Association Française pour l'Archéologie du Verre, 35-40

Guido, M. (1978) 'The Glass Beads of Prehistoric and Roman Periods in Britain and Ireland', *Report of the Research Committee of the Society of Antiquaries of London*, 35

Jackson, C., Cool, H., & Wager, E. (1998) 'The manufacture of Roman glass in York', *Journal of Glass Studies* **40**, 55-61

Price, J. (1998) 'The social context of glass production in Roman Britain', in McCray, P. (ed.) *The Prehistory and History of Glassmaking Technology*, Cincinnati, 331-48

Price, J. (2002) 'Broken bottles and quartz-sand: glass production in Yorkshire and the north in the Roman period', in P. Wilson & J. Price (eds) *Aspects of Industry in Roman Yorkshire and the North*, Oxbow Books

Price, J. & Cool, H. (1991) 'The evidence for the production of glass in Roman Britain', in D. Foy & Sennequier *Ateliers de Verriers de l'Antiquité à la période Pré-instrielle*. Rouen, l'Association Française pour l'Archéologie du Verre, 23-30

Price, J. & Cottam, S. (1998) *Romano-British Glass Vessel: A Handbook*. Council for British Archaeology

Shepherd, J. & Heyworth, M. (1991) 'Le travail du verre dans Londres romain (Londinium), un état de la question', in D. Foy & Sennequier *Ateliers de Verriers de l'Antiquité à la période Pré-instrielle*. Rouen, l'Association Française pour l'Archéologie du Verre, 13-22

3 A MEDIEVAL CRAFT 500–1500

Bayley, J. (2000) 'Glass-working in early medieval England', in Price, J. (ed.) *Glass in Britain and Ireland AD 350-1100*. British Museum Occasional Paper **127**, 137-43

Bayley, J. (2000) 'Saxon glass-working at Glastonbury Abbey', in Price, J. (ed.) *Glass in Britain and Ireland AD 350-1100*. British Museum Occasional Paper **127**, 161-88

Campbell, E. (2000) 'A review of glass vessels in western Britain and Ireland', in Price, J. (ed.) *Glass in Britain and Ireland AD 350-1100*. British Museum Occasional Paper **127**, 33-46

Cramp, R. (2000) 'Anglo-Saxon window glass', in Price, J. (ed.) *Glass in Britain and Ireland AD 350-1100*. British Museum Occasional Paper **127**, 105-114

Evison, V. (2000) 'Glass vessels in England, AD 400-1100', in Price, J. (ed.) *Glass in Britain and Ireland AD 350-1100*. British Museum Occasional Paper **127**, 47-104

Kenyon, G. (1967) *The Glass Industry of the Weald*. University of Leicester Press

Fossati, S. & Mannoni, T. (1975) 'Lo scavo della vetreria medievale di monte Lecco', *Archeologia Medievale* **2**, 31-97

Guido, M. (1999) 'The glass beads of Anglo-Saxon England, c.AD400-700: a preliminary visual classification of the more definitive and diagnostic types.' Report of the Research Committee of the Society of Antiquaries of London **58**

Guido, M. & Welsh, M. (2000) 'Indirect evidence for glass bead manufacture in early Anglo-Saxon England', in Price, J. (ed.) *Glass in Britain and Ireland AD 350-1100*. British Museum Occasional Paper **127**, 115-20

MacGowan, K. (1996) 'Barking Abbey'. *Current Archaeology* **149**, 172-78

Newstead, R. (1939) 'Glasshouse in Delamere Forest, Cheshire'. *Journal of the Chester and North Wales Archaeological Society* **33**, 32-9

O'Brien, C., (1997) 'Forest glass furnaces in County Offaly'. *Archaeology Ireland* **Vol. 11 No 4.**, 21-23

Pape, T. (1934) 'Medieval glassworkers in north Staffordshire'. *Transactions of the Staffordshire Field Club* **68**, 73-121

Tyson, R. (2000) 'Medieval Glass Vessels Found in England 1200-1500'. *CBA Research Report* **121**

Welch, C. (1997) 'Glass-making at Wolseley, Staffordshire'. *Post-Medieval Archaeology* **31**, 1-60

Winbolt, S. (1933) *Wealden Glass, the Surrey-Sussex Glass Industry AD 1226-1615*. Combridges

Wood, E. (1965) 'A medieval glasshouse at Blunden's Wood, Hambleton, Surrey'. *Sussex Archaeological Collections* **62**, 54-79

4 IMMIGRANTS AND ENTREPRENEURS 1500–1650

Baddeley, W. St Clair (1920) 'A glass house at Nailsworth'. *Transactions of the Bristol and Gloucester Archaeology Society* **42**, 89-95

Bridgewater, N. (1963) 'Glasshouse Farm, St Weonards: a small glassworking site'. *Woolhope Naturalists Field Club* **37**, 300-15

Crossley, D. (1967) 'Glassmaking in Bagot's Park'. *Post-Medieval Archaeology* **1**, 44-83

Crossley, D. (1987) 'Sir William Clavell's glasshouse at Kimmeridge, Dorset; the excavations of 1980-81'. *Archaeological Journal* **144**, 355-69

Crossley, D. (1994) 'The Wealden glass industry revisited'. *Industrial Archaeology Review* **17 No. 1**, 64-74

Crossley, D. & Aberg, A. (1972) 'Sixteenth-century glassmaking in Yorkshire, excavations at the furnaces of Hutton and Rosedale, North Riding, 1968-71'. *Post-Medieval Archaeology* **6**, 107-59

Daniels, J. (1950) *The Woodchester Glasshouse*. John Bellows Limited

Fox, R. & Lewis, E. (1982) 'William Overton and glassmaking in Buriton, an account of the sixteenth century glasshouse excavated in Ditcham Woods'. *Petersfield Historical Society Monographs* **1**

Godfrey, E. (1975) *The Development of English Glassmaking, 1560-1640*. Oxford University Press

Hurst-Vose, R. (1994) 'Excavations at the 17th Century Glasshouse at Haughton Green, Denton near Manchester'. *Post-Medieval Archaeology* **18**, 20-42

Hurst-Vose, R. (1995) 'Excavations at the *c.*1600 Bickerstaff Glasshouse, Lancashire'. *Merseyside Archaeology Society Journal* **9**, 1-24

Lennard, T. (1905) 'Glass-making at Knole, Kent'. *Antiquary* **41**, April. 127-9

Pape, T. (1934) 'Medieval glassworkers in north Staffordshire'. *Transactions of the Staffordshire Field Club* **68**, 73-121

Penn, H. (1983) 'Glassmaking in Gloucestershire'. *Journal of the Gloucestershire Society for Industrial Archaeology for 1983*, 3-16

Smith, R. (1962) 'Glassmaking at Wollaton in the early seventeenth century'. *Transactions of the Thoroton Society* **66**, 24-34

Sutton, A. & Sewell, J. (1980) 'Jacob Verzelini and the City of London'. *Glass Technology* **21 No. 4**, 190-2

Vince, A. (1977) 'Newent Glasshouse'. *Committee for Rescue Archaeology in Avon Gloucestershire and Somerset Occasional Paper 2*

Welch, C. (1997) 'Glass-making at Wolseley, Staffordshire'. *Post-Medieval Archaeology* **31**, 1-60

Willmott, H. (2002) 'Early post-medieval vessel glass in England, 1500-1670'. *CBA Research Report* **132**

Wood, E. 'A 16th century glasshouse at Knightons, Alford, Surrey'. *Surrey Archaeological Collections* **73**, 2-47

5 SCIENTISTS AND INDUSTRIALISTS 1650–1800

Ashurst, D. (1970) 'Excavations at Gawber Glasshouse, near Barnsley, Yorkshire'. *Post-Medieval Archaeology* **4**, 92–140

Ashurst, D. (1987) 'Excavations at the 17th-18th century Glasshouse at Bolsterstone and the 18th century Bolsterstone Pothouse, Stocksbridge, Yorkshire'. *Post-Medieval Archaeology* **21**, 147–226

Ashurst, D. (1992) *The History of South Yorkshire Glass*. JR Collis Publications

Boland, P. & Ellis, J. (1997) 'A Lost Stourbridge Glassworks Rediscovered'. *Journal of the Glass Association* **5**, 7–25

Buckley, F. (1915) *Old London Glasshouses*. Stevens & Sons

Charleston, R. (1984) *English glass and the glass used in England, 400-1900*. George Allen.

Crossley, D. (2003) 'The archaeology of the coal-fuelled glass industry in England'. *Archaeological Journal* **160**, 160–999

Ellis, J. (2002) *Glassmakers of Stourbridge and Dudley 1612-2002*. Xlibris

Francis, P. (2000) 'The development of lead glass'. *Apollo 151* (February 2000), 47–53

Hartshorne, A. (1968) *Antique Drinking Glasses, A Pictorial History of Glass Drinking Vessels*. 2nd ed. Brussel & Brussel, New York

Jackson, R. (2005) 'Excavations on the site of Sir Abraham Elton's glassworks, Cheese Lane, Bristol'. *Post-Medieval Archaeology* **30 pt1**, 92–132

Mackinder, A. & Bletherwick, S. (2000), 'Bankside. Excavations at Benbow House, Southwarl, London SE1'. *Museum of London Archaeology Service Study Series 3*

Moretti, C. (2004) 'The development of lead crystal in England'. *Revista della Stazione Sperimentale del Vetro* **34**, 28–32

RCHME (1997) 'Lemington Glass Cone, Newburn, Tyne and Wear. Historic Buildings Report', Royal Commission on the Historical Monuments of England

Smith, A. (2004) 'The Nailsea Glassworks, Nailsea, North Somerset. A Study of the History, Archaeology, Technology and the Human Story'. *http://ads.ahds.ac.uk/catalogue/library/nailsea_avon_2004*

Torsten & Berg, P. (2001) *R.R. Angerstein's Illustrated Travel Diary, 1753-1755 : Industry in England and Wales from a Swedish Perspective*. The Science Museum

Tyler, K. & Willmott, H. (2005) 'John Baker's late 17th-century glasshouse at Vauxhall'. Museum of London Archaeology Service Monograph **28**

Weeden, C. (1983) 'The Bristol glass industry: its rise and decline'. *Glass Technology* **24**, 241–58

Witt, C., Weeden, C. & Schwind, A. (1984) 'Bristol Glass'. City of Bristol Museum and Art Gallery

POSTSCRIPT: THE NINETEENTH CENTURY

Hollister, P. (1995) 'Europe and America 1800-1940', in Tait, H. (ed.) *Five Thousand Years of Glass*. British Museum Press, 188-210

Krupa, M. & Heawood, R. (2002) *The Hotties' Excavation and building survey at Pilkingtons' No 9 Tank House St Helens, Merseyside*. Lancaster Imprints

Newby, M. (2003) *From Palace to Parlour, a celebration of 19th-century British Glass*. Balding & Mansell Ltd

INDEX

This index covers the principal sites and individuals discussed in the text. Page numbers in **bold** refer to illustrations.

If you are interested in purchasing other books published by Tempus,
or in case you have difficulty finding any Tempus books in your local bookshop,
you can also place orders directly through our website

www.tempus-publishing.com